Sandy's Miracle

God Bless
Patsy Giddings

Sandy's Miracle

Patsy Giddings
&
John Borgstedt

authorHOUSE®

AuthorHouse™
1663 Liberty Drive
Bloomington, IN 47403
www.authorhouse.com
Phone: 1-800-839-8640

Published by AuthorHouse   01/25/2013

ISBN: 978-1-4817-0611-7 (sc)
ISBN: 978-1-4817-0610-0 (hc)
ISBN: 978-1-4817-0651-3 (e)

Library of Congress Control Number: 2013900688

DEDICATION

I dedicate this book First and Foremost to God:

You gave me the precious gift of life

And then taught me to appreciate it

I live for your honor and glory.

I also dedicate this book to my husband

And children

Thank you, for all your love, support

And understanding

I love you all.

ACKNOWLEDGMENTS

This book is written with special thanks to:

- My husband Mark,for your love,understanding,total support of all my dreams. for the outstanding job you did on taking the cover picture of my book. And most of all, for being my soulmate,I love you honey.

- My children, Jonathon, Amanda, and Rebecca, you are the sources of my greatest joy, and my life would be empty without each of you in it, thank you for all your love, support and encouragement through the years.

- My granddaughter Elizabeth, for allowing me to use your picture for the cover of my book.

- David Ayers, for caring, believing in me, and initiating the writing of this book, which would not exist, had it not been for you, thank you from the bottom of my heart.

- Chris Mullens, for your professionalism, patience, endless hours of help and encouragement, for pushing me and being my voice when I needed one. I couldn't have written this book without you.

- My CASA "family", Johnnie Wheeler, Judy Greenwood, Rita Turnipseed, Rondi Van Vorce, for all your encouragement, support and most importantly your friendship.

- Jennifer Kelly, L.C.S.W, for your unconditional love and encouragement, for helping me to accept and overcome my childhood abuse, and for accepting me just as I am, God truly blessed me when he brought you into my life, thank you dear friend for your tireless efforts.

- Sue Fredrick, for your generous spirit, encouragement, and our lunch dates; I am so blessed to have your friendship.

- Dr. Richard H. Wearing, for the interest you've shown and the encouragement you've given, thank you.

- Jennifer Stainbrook, Randi Thomas, for your support, friendship and always lending a helping hand when I needed one.

- David Giddings, for all the love, support, and help that you gave me through the years, thank you from the bottom of my heart.

- Pat Thomas, for your editing skills which allowed this book to be published.

- Manhattan Beauty Salon, thank you Jennifer Brown and Shannon Lee, for your creative talents in hair and makeup and the wonderful look you gave me for my picture.

- Willard Cantrell, for the outstanding pictures you photographed for my book.

- And to the Lord, for His constant inspiration, guidance, and unconditional love…

Thank you all for making this book possible

MY PRAYER

Heavenly Father, creator of the universe, and everything in it, I humbly approach your unreachable throne at this time, to thank you for the privilege and honor of being used as your instrument, to glorify you and Your Son, Jesus. I thank you for the opportunity that's been given me, to be a voice for the abused and neglected children of the world. Thank you for the sweet precious life and many blessings you have given me throughout my life. Father in Heaven, You are the master Author of the greatest book ever written, "The Bible," so I humbly pray for your guidance, direction and blessing in the writing of my book. I pray this prayer in Jesus Holy name. AMEN!

CONTENTS

CHAPTER ONE

MY EARLIEST MEMORIES

I sit on the sofa in my living room, with a cup of coffee in reach, and my computer on my lap. My four Toy Chihuahua dogs have surrounded me, one on each side, and the other two laying across my neck. I am now about to embark on the story of my life's journey, and expose to the world, the deep dark hidden secrets of my past. I pray God will bring back to my memory, the severe childhood abuse I struggled so hard, my whole life to forget.

I was born in Los Angeles, CA. My parents named me Sandra Gene, and gave me the nick name *Sandy*. Shortly after I was born, my parents moved our family to Lansing, MI, where we lived in an upstairs duplex apartment. My family consisted of my parents, one brother and two sisters. My siblings and I shared a bedroom and at bedtime, we would all sleep on the same bare mattress. We had few toys to play with and very few clothes to wear.

When Uncle Chester, my daddy's brother, would come to visit, he would find us kids, many times not wearing shoes, or coats, while playing outside in the winter snow. Yes, my family was very poor, but my siblings and I were too young to know or care.

Both my parents were unstable, uneducated, and had no parenting or money management skills. Instead of buying food for the family, my mother would spend her food stamps on drinking and partying. My daddy's pay checks never made it home either, like my mother, his money was spent on drinking and eating out. With all this said about my parents though, I can still say I loved them both very much. I was far too young to realize they were not being good parents, so in my heart I had the best parents in the world.

Some of my earliest memories, at about the *age of four*, are of good times spent with my "Uncle Bob", my mother's brother and his wife, "Aunt Marie." Uncle Bob and Aunt Marie had five children of their own and frequently would take my siblings and me on extended visits to their home. Uncle Bob and Aunt Marie knew that mother and daddy were not taking care of us, and were very concerned for our wellbeing. I recall a time while on a visit with them, Uncle Bob picked me up, and put me in his lap while he was eating. He began to feed me from his plate and with a big smile on his face, he asked me if I was his little girl and I replied, "Yes, uh-huh". Of course at that moment *I felt just like a princess!*

I also remember a time, when my mother came home from grocery shopping, and called us kids into the kitchen for a bowl of ice cream. The minute I heard ice cream, I began to jump up and down with sheer joy, and ran as fast as I could to her side. Yes, I can truly say, the memories I have of living with my family, at the most tender and innocent years of my childhood are like having precious gold.

"I have etched them deep in my heart and soul never to be erased!"

I had a mother and daddy that I loved very much and a brother and two sisters to play with. In my four year old mind, I was happy and life was good! But little did I know my life and everything in it was about to change forever.

I was told years later, while mother would be out partying and drinking, that she would leave us kids home alone, or with whomever she could get to babysit us. I remember waking up one night, and daddy sitting on the side of my bed. Startled at the sound I heard, I sat straight up in the bed, and said "What's wrong daddy? Are you okay?" "I'm okay Sandy," he said to me, "Lie down and go back to sleep." So I laid my head back down on the mattress, but again, I heard that same startling sound, and saw daddy vomiting on the floor. This frightened me so much, that I began to cry. "Sandy, why are you crying?" daddy asks. As I stretched out my arms in hopes that daddy would pick me up, I cried out to him, *I am scared, daddy!* He then turned around, lifted me up and ever so gently cradled me in his arms. He said, *"Don't cry baby girl, daddy will be okay."* Then he very softly began to rock and sing to me. *"Hush baby girl, your daddy's here".*

Up to this day, I can still feel the gentleness of daddy's arms, holding me snug to his chest. Hear the soothing sound of his voice in my ears as he sang to me. At that very moment, *daddy was my hero!* For just a little while, time stood still for me to embrace my daddy's love. Sadly though, that one precious moment in time would be my last to see my daddy for years to come. I have kept and cherished the memory of that night my entire life.

Then suddenly! Daddy and I heard what sounded like thunder, but really was someone's feet stomping up the stairs of our duplex apartment. "Daddy, who is that," I said, and daddy mumbled under his breath, "It's your mother. She's been down stairs at the neighbor's. There was a party down there and she left you kid's home alone again."

When mother reached the top of the stairs, she began yelling, "Where have you been Charles?" Evidently, daddy must have left the house to go drinking, before mother left to go to her shindig down stairs. Daddy came home before mother did and he was upset at mother for leaving us kids alone, so he too was angry.

By the time my mother made it to my bedroom, she was very mad at daddy and really lashed out at him. As she came into the room she stepped on daddy's vomit and fell to the floor. Instantly, I went into a state of panic. I had never seen or heard my parents argue before, at least that I could remember, so I was terrified of what was going to happen next. At first she was livid and blamed daddy for her fall. Then she began laughing at herself and told daddy, "You better clean this mess up, Thomas!" Still clinging to daddy's arms, he laid me back down on the bed. The hall light my mother had turned on shined into my dark bedroom and as I drifted back off to sleep, I watched my daddy on his hands and knees, cleaning up his own vomit off the floor. *This would be my last memory of him as a little girl.*

Sometime in the night, after I had fallen back to sleep, mother had someone come to the apartment to babysit us kids while she took daddy to the hospital. When I awakened the next morning, daddy was gone and mother never spoke to us kids about his absence. At four years old you have no concept of time, so daddy being gone didn't affect me much at that time.

A couple of years later I was told that after daddy was discharged from the hospital, he and mother tried to work their problems out in hopes of keeping our family together, but sadly their efforts failed. Daddy then returned to the hospital and he would stay there for an extended period of time.

CHAPTER TWO

INNOCENTS IOST

After daddy had been readmitted into the hospital, my mother's boyfriend, Fred, who lived in the downstairs apartment, moved in with us. At times when mother would leave the apartment, she would have Fred babysit us kids.

I remember a time when mother had planned to go somewhere, and she asked Fred to babysit. While Fred was preoccupied watching TV, my siblings and I decided to go down stairs to the front porch of the apartment. We were all sitting on the porch, when suddenly we heard a loud thumping sound in the stairwell. Marcia, our eighteen month old baby sister, had just fallen down the stairs. When she reached the bottom step, her legs were bleeding and she was screaming and crying. I was sure Fred would have heard her cries and would come to get her, but he didn't.

I knew Marcia would be too heavy for me to carry. I was very small for my age and due to being neglected, I was malnourished and frail, but I knew I had to help her. I went behind Marcia and placed my arms around her body and under her arms. I then, with all my strength, picked the top portion of her body up and dragged her to the porch steps. I sat down and pulled her body across my lap. I then looked around on the porch for anything I could use to clean her legs, but there was nothing there.

"Janet, will you go upstairs and get a rag?," I asked my older sister. Janet agreed to go, and a few minutes later, came back with a towel. I then began cleaning Marcia's legs, while trying to comfort her and letting her know that she would be okay. Fred must have noticed Janet getting a towel and by that time heard Marcia crying, and he came looking for us. Like a raging bull, he stormed down the stairs and sounding like a mama bear ready to attack to protect her cubs, he shouted, *"I'm going to beat all of you."*

Fred had not been in my life long enough at that point for me to have established any kind of relationship with him, but I never forgot what kind of man he was after that day, and I always made sure I kept a safe distance from him.

He reached the porch, jerked Marcia out of my arms and yelled at me, "What did you do to her?" I began to cry and said, "I didn't do anything to her. Marcia fell, following us down the stairs, and I was trying to help her. He yells again, "Get up those stairs, all of you, get to the kitchen, and when you get there, pull your pants down, get in one line and stand there until I call your name, for your turn, to get beat by the end of my belt. I started crying even harder and ask him, "Why are we getting a beating?" Fred yells at me, "Because you were on this porch and it's your fault Marcia fell."

In total fear and desperation, all I could think about at that moment was to somehow change his mind. I tried pleading and begging, as I cried my heart out to him, *"Please don't beat me, please don't beat me! I'm sorry, I won't do it again!* We weren't going to leave the porch. I didn't know Marcia would follow us. All I did was pick her up after she fell and wipe the blood off her legs."

Sad to say, all my pleading, crying and begging did not change Fred's sadistic mind set. Fred made sure I was the first of my siblings to feel the horrific pain of his steel belt buckle on my bare bottom and the back of my legs. The severe pain from that beating lingered on for hours and so did my sobbing! Mother and daddy had never whipped me that I could remember, but this beating would be one that I would never forget, and it would be just the beginning of many more to come.

Anything would put Fred on the war path, and when it did, we were always ordered like little soldiers to go to the kitchen, pull our pants down, stand in one line, shoulders straight, and mouth shut, or the beating would be worse. We were so young, so vulnerable and innocent! We couldn't have known that Fred had plans for Janet and me far beyond our imagination. The beatings would be just a prelude of what was to come!

Mother had company one night, and when they arrived she sent us kids to bed. Like all young children do, we played for a while, and then went to sleep. Sometime in the middle of the night, I was awakened by someone's hand on me. I turned over in the bed to see who was touching me. To my surprise, Fred was standing next to my bed. "What are you doing?," I asked him. "You're too old to be sleeping with us." Fred just smiled and said to me, "It's ok, Sandy. Your mommy said I could."

I don't like you touching me. I cried and threatened him, "I'm telling my mommy." "Yes, and if you do, I will beat you with my belt," he harshly snapped at me. At four years old, I knew Fred being in my room was wrong, and I didn't understand why he was touching me.

The child spirit inside me, so pure and innocent, vanished. Fred stole my innocence like a thief in the night.

My tiny, frail, body seemed to go limp, out of *complete terror!* I felt my mind leave my body and it seemed like I was floating above the bed. When I looked down, I saw someone else, "I *was okay," because it wasn't me!* That night forever enlightened me on how cruel Fred could be, and how life wasn't the fairy tale I thought it was. After that night Fred haunted me in my nightmares for many years to come.

My mind then reflected back on the horrific pain I felt from Fred's belt buckle, and I kept this horrible secret to myself. The visits from Fred, in the middle of the night, continued until we left our family home. Out of fear of him, none of us kids ever told my mother about what Fred was doing

CHAPTER THREE

STATE CUSTODY

The length of time that passed by, from receiving Fred's daily beatings and middle of the night visits to our bedroom, *is like the morning fog to my memory. You know something is in the fog, but no matter how hard you try, you just can't see through it.*

I can only assume that mother was gone from home a lot, or at that point in her life, she simply didn't care. Then to my surprise, the day of salvation came, or at least I thought it was. But instead, it would be just a continuation of the same abuse, only worse!

The neighbor who lived across the street from our home, contacted DCS. She stated to them that she had watched my mother get into a cab with her suitcase in hand, and then the cab drove away. The neighbor also stated that she had seen my brother John in the alley many times, digging through the garbage for food. The neighbor explained to the police that she was concerned that we had been abandoned.

When DCS and the police came to our home to pick us kids up, I was lying on the mattress, burning up with fever. I could hear the pounding on the front door, but I was too sick to move off the mattress, and I knew one of my other siblings would answer the door. When they came into the apartment all of us kids were dirty, hungry and wearing nothing more than underwear and tee shirts. I was too young to know who these people were or why they were in our home, but I do remember the kindness and warmth they showed us kids. They washed our little bodies, and replaced the smelly, dirty clothes we were wearing, with clean ones, before taking us away.

I really can't recall if my mother was there that day, but as they started out the front door to take us to their cars, *frantically*, I quickly spoke up and told these people, "My mommy says we can't go with strangers." The officer picked me up in his arms, and while carrying me to his car, told me that my mommy said it was okay.

In my mind, these nice people were going to take us kids for a ride in the car and then take us right back home.

There were several unmarked police and DCS cars parked in front of our home. I was placed in the first car and John, Janet and Marcia were put in the car directly behind me. I remember thinking how special I was, because I had been given my own car, and my siblings had to share a car. I turned around in my car seat and looked out the back window. I smiled and waved at my siblings with pure delight as we all drove away.

I had no clue that it would be the last time for me to see my baby sister Marcia, and it would be 26 years before I would see my brother John again.

CHAPTER FOUR

EMOTIONAL AND MENTAL ABUSE

I was at a very fragile and delicate age when I was taken from my family. To make things worse, because I was sick, I was taken straight to a hospital to be checked out. There was no explanation given to me as to why I was being taken to a hospital, or why my siblings weren't brought along with me. Simply put, *I was just taken!*

Because I was not taken back home after the car ride, I thought these people that I had never seen before, complete and total strangers to me, had just stolen me from my mother. Not knowing when, or if ever, I would see my mother and siblings again, was mentally and very emotionally traumatizing to me.

When we arrived at the hospital, I was carried in, taken to an exam room and made to sit down on a cold table. A nurse came into the room, and started to examine me. I asked, "Why are you looking at me like this? Where is my mommy? Is my mommy coming?" The nurse smiled and said, "Because you are sick, Sandy, we need to examine you to make sure you're okay, and yes, your mommy will be here later." About that time two more nurses came into the room, and while standing at the doorway, they were discussing my case along with what health issues I had at the time. Of course, I didn't understand much of what they were saying, but when one of the nurses spoke up and said, *"Here's one that's not going to live very long." I was stunned!* Surprisingly, I understood that statement, and when it sank in my mind what she had just said, it hit me like a ton of bricks. I became extremely upset and began to cry. Somehow, at that moment, I knew she was talking about my physical life.

For years it was beyond my comprehension how I could have known, at such a young age, what life or death meant. But after finding in the *Bible* the scripture below, I then understood and have come to realize that *"GOD, Our Heavenly Father," has created mankind with the desire to live forever!*

He has made everything beautiful in its time. He has also set eternity in the hearts of men; yet they cannot fathom what God has done from beginning to end

ECC 3:11 (NIV)

"What's wrong, why are you crying Sandy?" The nurse taking care of me asked. With tears falling down my cheeks, and thoughts racing through my mind that I would never grow up, I managed to get out of my mouth, *"Because I don't want to die."* She then asked me, "What do you mean, Sandy, do you know what the word die means?" "It means I won't be alive anymore. I will be dead and I don't want to die," I said to her as I sat there sobbing. "Who told you that you were going to die," she asked? I glanced over toward the door where the two nurses were standing and pointed to the nurse that had made the comment. "Did she tell you that you were going to die?," the nurse asked. I said, "No, but I heard her tell the lady standing next to her that I wouldn't live very long."

The nurse said, "Sandy, honey, you're not going to die." I looked up at her and said, "Then why did that lady say that about me, what's wrong with me?" She then very calmly and slowly began to explain to me that I was born with a heart condition and at that time it couldn't be fixed. Still sobbing as I blurted out to her, *"Why can't you fix me?"* She replied, "Medicine hasn't come that far yet, to fix the kind of heart condition you have." *"Then I am going to die," I yelled back at her.* She put her arms around me and softly said, "Honey," the kind of heart condition you have doesn't mean that you're going to die while you're still a little girl. You just may not live to a real old age. "What's an old age?," I asked. She smiled and said, "Oh, you should live to be at least fifty or sixty years old, and don't you worry, because that's still pretty old." She also said, "Maybe by the time you get to be around that age the doctors will have found a way to fix your heart, so stop crying, okay, you're going to be just fine."

Needless to say, after the nurse had finished with my exam, she immediately turned to the nurse that had upset me, and gave her a good talking to. Unfortunately though, the damage had been done, and nothing was going to erase what she had said from my mine. I felt I was in a nightmare and couldn't wake up. I was so overwhelmed at that moment with feelings of loneliness. I wanted and desperately needed my mother to be there to comfort me, but she wasn't. My heart throbbed and ached at the thought that I may not live to grow old. I never forgot what was said that day, or how I felt. Those memories have stayed with me throughout my entire life and to beat it all she was right. As it turns out, I was born with a heart birth defect, but it wouldn't be detected until years later.

After the nurse had calmed me down and had finished with my exam, she then took me to my hospital room. I glanced around the room hoping to get a glimpse of my mother being there; when instead I noticed a baby bed and wondered why it was in my room. My first thought was, I'm not a baby. I don't sleep in a baby bed. My mind then focused back on my mother still not being there. "Where's my mommy, I want to see my mommy," I repeated several times to the nurse. "Oh she'll be here," the nurse said as she was undressing me to put my hospital clothes on. After I was dressed I was taken down the hall to the nurses' station and offered something to eat, but I was too scared and missing my mother so much that I couldn't eat. I remember some nurses coming over to me and trying to bribe me with ice-cream just to get me to eat, but it seemed all I could do was cry.

Realizing that I was not going to eat, a nurse picked me up and carried me back to my hospital room. Before she put me to bed she started to put a diaper on me. I got even more upset and tried telling her that I wasn't a baby and I didn't wear diapers or sleep in a baby bed. As she struggled to keep me still so she could put the diaper on me she said, "It's okay Sandy, you need to be still, I know you're not a baby, but we don't want you to fall out of the bed and we are putting the diaper on you in case you have an accident in the middle of the night." Still crying I said to her, "I don't wet the bed; I'm not a baby."

I was so embarrassed! I couldn't believe, I was being treated as if I was my baby sister Marcia. *"Mommy, where are you? Please come get me,"* I thought to myself. I knew if my mother was there, she would tell them that I wasn't a baby. I may have only been four years old at the time, but my feelings and pride were deeply hurt! The nurse then put me to bed and I cried myself to sleep.

Sometime the next day, a nurse came into my hospital room, reached for my hand and said, "Come with me Sandy, we need to go down the hall to another room for a few minutes." "Have you seen my mommy?" I said to her as I took her hand and we walked down the corridor of the hospital floor that my room was on. "No, she said, but I'm sure you will see her soon." I saw three nurses in the room when we walked in. One was sitting in a chair and the other two were standing beside her.

Now keep in mind, I had no clue as to what was getting ready to happen.

The nurse that had walked me down the hall then said to me, "Come here, Sandy, you need to pull your pajama bottoms down and lie across this lady's lap for a minute." I totally did not understand what was going on. I knew pulling my pants down was not going to be a good thing because of the beatings from

Fred and his nightly visits to my bedroom. Not knowing what to expect, I was very reluctant to let them do anything with me. But of course being a little girl, it's not like I had any choice in the matter.

As they grabbed hold of my body and pulled me over to the nurse that was sitting down on the chair, *I began to scream and cry out, "Where's my mommy! I want my mommy!"* I tried as hard as I could to jerk away from them, but my tiny sick body was no match for four grown women. Once laid across the nurse's lap, within seconds I felt a sharp stabbing pain and then even more pain, as the medicine from the needle was injected into my bottom end. *I cried and screamed as loud as I could, "Mommy, mommy, I want my mommy!"* I struggled and kicked with all my might, but was not able to free myself from their grip. All I could think about was how bad the pain was, and what are they doing to me? Over and over in my mind I kept thinking, *"Mommy where are you, please mommy come get me!"* A few seconds later I was given a second injection on the other side of my bottom. Of course, the pain was worse yet because I could still feel the pain from the first injection. Again, I screamed and cried and pled for my mother to be there.

None of the authorities, or medical staff explained to me why I had been taken from my mother and siblings, or why I needed injections while being in the hospital. So by this time in my mind, *I had been stolen, had my heart broken, had my feelings and pride hurt, and now violated, tortured and lied to.*

I have not been able to recover my medical records since my adoption, so I don't know the name of the hospital, or how long I was there, but I do remember the nurse, on two different occasions, coming to my hospital room and taking me to that same room to get shots.

As I think back to my last day in the hospital, I remember the nurse walking into my room and instantly my thought was, "Oh no, not again!" She was coming to take me for more shots, so naturally, dreading another round of pain, I began to cry. But this time was different. Instead of taking my hand and walking me down the corridor to receive my injections, like she had done two times before, she first dressed me into the clothes I was wearing, when I was brought into the hospital.

I knew I hadn't been made to change into my clothes when having injections before that day, so I did question in my mind why the nurse was having me change this time, but my focus and concern at that moment was more on having to take yet another set of shots, and then having to deal with the pain they would cause, once again!

I was still upset so I cried the whole time the nurse was dressing me. "Why are you crying, Sandy?," she asked. I said, "Because I don't want more shots." She then looked at me and with a big warm smile on her face and said, "You're leaving the hospital today Sandy, so don't be upset. You don't have to take any more shots. Isn't that great?"

Because I had been so traumatized by everything that had happened to me while in their care at the hospital, I wasn't able to trust anyone or believe anything that was told to me. I had been lied to the whole time I was there, so I asked again! "Are you sure I don't have to have more shots today? Are you taking me back home to my mommy now? Is my mommy coming to get me now? The nurse replied, "Sandy, your mommy is having some problems and you aren't going to be able to be with her for a while, but there is a real nice lady that came here to the hospital just to meet you. She will be taking you to a foster home, where you will stay for a while, until you can be with your mommy again." "What is a Foster Home? Will my brother and sister's be there? Are the people there nice? When will I get to see my mommy?" I asked. Although the nurse answered all my questions to the best of her ability, I was still scared of not knowing what would happen next.

This was the first time throughout my whole hospital stay, which to me was like a nightmare that had no ending that anyone cared enough to give me an explanation as to why *my whole life and everything in it had just been taken away from me*. At that moment, I was terrified out of my mind at the thought of living with strange people I had never met before, and being away from my siblings, but at least I finally had some answers.

This is a picture of my biological father after
we had reunited twenty-five years later.

This is a picture of my biological mother
that was sent to me in a letter.

This is one of three pictures that I have
of myself when I was in foster care.

This is a picture of my son Jonathon and his family.
Front (L-R): McKenna & Gavin,
Middle (L-R): Jonathan & Jennifer
Back: (L-R)Tyler, Alexes, Keaton

This is a picture of my youngest daughter, Rebecca
and her family. Front (L-R): Brian and Brieanna
Back (L-R): Greg and Rebecca

This is a picture of my oldest daughter Amanda

This is a picture of Mark and I being sworn in,
by judge Hudson, as CASA Volunteers.
From left to right Rita Turnipseed, Mark Giddings,
Me, Judge Hudson, Jeremy Sauer, Bill Sorrell

This is a picture of me with Senator Charlotte Burks,
when I attended the Children's Advocacy Days,
in Nashville, TN on March 14, 2012.
From left to right Judy Greenwood, Rita
Turnipseed, John Rust, Me, Senator Charlotte
Burks, Carolyn Isbell, Rondi R. Van Vorce

This is a picture of me giving a lecture at
the TN CASA Network Training/Director's
Meeting, in Murfreesboro, TN May 3, 2012.

Patsy,

Hello my love; my best friend!

You know, it's hard sometimes to put in
words or express in feelings, how you
really feel about someone. At times you
think I don't mean a single word I say.

REMBER ONLY ONE THING

*"Their only words and words are all I have
To take your heart away"*

When you call me or need me, "I'll be there." *GOD*
brought us together to make us stronger and better
human beings. Our children, grandchildren, foster
children, and grandchildren to come need us.

LOVE is a magical and powerful word but
it can also destroy lives. Never have a
stoned heart; keep an open mind.
As husband and wife, if we stick together and
respect each other, *we can accomplish ANYTHING!!*

SOUL MATES FOREVER...

Your devoted husband and friend,
Mark

23

CHAPTER FIVE

FOSTER CARE

After I left the hospital, I lived in four different foster homes. These are my experiences of being in Foster Care.

First Foster Home:

Ms. Smith, the Social Worker that had been assigned my case, was waiting for me at the nurses' station on the morning that I was released from the hospital. She greeted me with a warm, caring smile and said, "Hi, Sandy, my name is Ms. Smith and I am your Social Worker. She reached out her hand for me to take hold of and softly said, "You have to come with me now, Sandy. I'm going to take you to your new foster home." I was happy to be leaving the hospital, so I had no reservation in going with her, but I was still terrified of having to go live with people I had never met and didn't know.

When we arrived at my first foster home, I was so afraid of being left there; I wouldn't get out of the car. Ms. Smith then came around to my side of the car, reached inside and took me out. As she carried me to the door I said, "Ms. Smith, please don't make me stay here. Why can't I go with you?" "Sandy, I am your Social Worker. I'm not allowed to take you home with me," she replied. These are really nice people; you will like them you'll see.

When we arrived at the door, Ms. Smith put me down and I stood glued to her side while she pressed the side doorbell to the foster parent's home. Within seconds of Ms. Smith ringing their doorbell, I could hear voices and then footsteps of someone walking toward the door. While standing there in total fear, not knowing who or what was waiting for me behind that door, I could feel my heart pounding and just knew that at any second it would jump right out of my chest. I wanted desperately to run away, but I felt like my legs were paralyzed and wouldn't move an inch. I was looking down at the ground, when the door opened and the first thing I saw was a pair of shoes. As my eyes scrolled up the foster dad's legs, then his body, I thought to myself, *I must be looking at a giant,* because it took so long for me to finally see his face. In reality the foster dad was a very nice man who just happen to be exceptionally tall, but in my mind I was looking at *a scary, giant monster that was about to eat me.* Instantly I started crying and screaming at the top of my lungs in *complete terror.* Ms. Smith quickly picked me up and stepped inside the house. Once inside, it was like I had a death grip around her neck, as if my life depended on it, and nothing was going to pry me loose.

I had never been so afraid in my entire life and have never been that afraid since!

Once inside the foster parent's home, both Ms. Smith and the foster parents tried to console me, but I was inconsolable. The foster mother tried taking me from Ms. Smith's arms, but I was wrapped around her neck and holding on for dear life. I was screaming, *"Please, Ms. Smith don't leave me here, I'm scared, please take me with you,"* as I clung to her neck! Ms. Smith then did the only thing she knew to do with me and that was take me to their living room and set me down in a chair. She then said, "It's okay, Sandy, I'm not leaving for a while. You just sit right here in this chair while I talk to your foster parents."

While sitting in the living room chair, I managed to stop crying, but couldn't believe what happen next. The GIANT MONSTER *(foster dad)*, walked into the room and sat in a chair directly across from where I'm seated, and started to read a newspaper. All though my fear had subsided somewhat, I still wasn't about to take my eyes off of him *(just in case I needed to run)*.

He sat there for a while reading his paper and then with no warning at all, he stood up with his newspaper in his hand and walked over to my chair. I'm thinking, "Oh no, what's he getting ready to do to me now" But instead of *devouring me, like most monster's do,* he bent down, offered me the paper and then said, "Sandy, would you like to read the newspaper?" After the initial shock of not being eaten and still having all my body parts had worn off, I said with a quivery voice, "I don't know how to read." The foster dad then smiled at me and said, "That's okay, Sandy, but you can still look at the pictures in the paper if you want to." At that point, I really had no desire to be looking at anything other than watching him, and besides, I needed to keep my focus on my surroundings in case I would need to protect myself.

Shortly after the foster dad had offered me the newspaper, Ms. Smith walked into the room and said to me, "Sandy, I have to leave now, don't be scared. These nice people are going to take care of you for awhile. I promise they are not going to hurt you. You will be fine". I wanted so desperately to follow behind Ms. Smith as she was leaving, but I knew I had no say in the matter and I would have to stay.

I'm not sure how much time had gone by, after being brought to this foster home, but I just couldn't seem to get a grip on my situation. I missed my family so much that I was literally grieving over the loss of them in my life. I was so grief-stricken that I refused to eat and would do nothing but cry every day. Concerned for my wellbeing, DCS brought my older sister Janet to stay with me for awhile, hoping that she would comfort me and help me to accept and to adjust to not being with my family.

I remember being so thrilled when I saw Janet. I hugged and kissed her and told her how much I had missed being with her and the rest of our siblings. I then asked, "How long will you get to stay with me, Janet?" She replied, "I don't know, Sandy, but let's not think about that now, let's go play". Janet was right; it was time to stop crying and time to start having fun with my sister again.

Janet and I really enjoyed each other's company. Every day we would laugh and play the same way we did before we were taken from our home and placed in State Custody. Although it never left our minds that our being together was only a quick fix for my heartbreak and loneliness of being separated from my family. It was always in the back of both our minds that the day would come that DCS would come and take her away from me again, and that day would come a lot sooner than either one of us wanted.

When Janet's Social Worker came to take her away from me again, we neither one had been told that it would be our last day to be together. I remember vividly the Social Worker coming to the foster home that day and telling us that it was time for Janet to leave because she had to go to her new foster home. Instantly, that same feeling of grief and loneliness came rushing back inside me like a huge waterfall and it consumed my whole body. Janet and I both began to cry and pleaded to the Social Worker not to take her, but our crying and pleading was all in vain. Janet was leaving and nothing was going to stop that!

After the foster mom and Social Worker had packed all of Janet's belongings, they loaded the Social Worker's car and then gave Janet and me a few minutes together to say our goodbys. As we hugged and held on ever so tightly to each other, we cried and told each other how much we loved one another and didn't want to be separated. I remember so plainly Janet and me telling ourselves that we knew we were not going to see each other again. After we stopped holding on to one another, I held Janet's hands and as I was crying my heart out, I said,

"Janet, I know we're not going to see each other again, but I promise no matter what happens, someday when we grow up, somehow, I will find you again, I PROMISE!"

It didn't seem long after Janet was taken from my foster home that for unknown reasons to me, I too was taken from that home and was placed in my second foster home.

Second Foster Home:

I have very little memory of this home, so I can only assume that I didn't live there very long. The one memory, though, that did stay with me throughout my life, and is the most important one of all, is the memory of *learning who God was for the first time.*

In this foster home one of their family members was getting married and wanted me to be a flower girl in their wedding. Before I was allowed to go to their church and be a part of their special day, I was sat down and talked to by one of the ladies in the family. She was giving me instructions about my role in the wedding, and also letting me know how I was expected to act throughout the occasion. She told me the wedding would be held in church, which was God's house, and that I was to be on my best behavior.

Not ever hearing about God before that day, naturally my first question was, *"Who is God?"* The lady answered my question by saying, "He's our creator, the one who made us, and He loves us very much." *"What is a God?* Where does God live?," I asked. She eagerly replied, "God is our Heavenly Father, and he lives high in the sky, far beyond all the clouds and the stars that are in the whole universe in a place called Heaven." "Can we go see him? I asked. She smiled and said, "No honey, but when we die, if we have done God's will, He will take us home to be with him in Heaven and we will see him then." I was so Intrigued at how a person could be alive, but yet humans could not see him in the flesh or go visit him at his home in Heaven, that it made me want to know even more about him.

The wedding day came and I made sure to do my best at being their flower girl. I was very young, but I knew that this was a very special day, not just because two people were getting married, but also because *I was in God's house, a place I had never been before*. I knew the lady who talked with me, before that day, had said we couldn't see God in the flesh but still in my mind, I was hoping he would be there so I could meet him.

I'm not sure how much time had gone by after the wedding day that I was told I would be moving to yet another foster home. Like most things in my life, at least up to that point, I was not given a reason why. *I was just taken!*

Third Foster Home:

By this point I was starting to get used to being shuffled from one foster home to another. I was toughening up, so to speak, but nothing I had already lived through would prepare me for the worst abuse that was yet to come!

When I was placed in this foster home I was about five years old at the time. My first memory of abuse in this home started on a day that I was sitting on a swing set in the back yard. I felt so sad and alone, wanting desperately to be back with my family again. As I sat there swinging slowly back and forth my mind drifted back to the times I had shared with my sister Janet, and thinking how we always had so much fun laughing and playing together. I longed for those days to be back again, but I knew in my heart that wasn't going to happen. I had finally accepted, at this point, that my life was continuing on without my parents and siblings. I wanted so much to have someone or something to play with that could help fill the *deep, agonizing feelings of emptiness inside me*. All little girls should have toy's and friends to play with, but because I was a State child, and moved from one foster home to another, *I had neither!*

Then to my surprise I suddenly heard a dog barking. I looked to see where the barking sound was coming from, and I spotted the foster parent's small dog in the back yard with me. My first thought on seeing the dog was, "Oh, good! Now I have something to play with." I don't remember the dog's name, but I called him over to me, so I could pick him up. I knew he was small and could get hurt very easily, so I made sure when picking him up, that I was very careful not to drop him. I then placed him in my lap and while I held him safely tucked under one arm, I began to slowly swing with him.

Evidently, the foster mom had been brushing her hair while watching me from a window inside the house. When I picked her dog up, it made her furious with me and she began yelling at me through the window, "Sandy, you bring me that dog right now, and I do mean now!" I could tell by the loud, screeching sound of her voice that I was in major trouble.

Not wanting to make her even angrier, I wasted no time carrying the dog in the house to her. She was so mad at me for picking up her dog, that she grabbed me by the hair of the head, jerked my pants down and started beating me with the wire hairbrush she had been using to brush her hair. "You get up those stairs right now, you little brat," she screamed at me, as she dragged and beat me all the way to the staircase. Naturally, due to the severe pain I felt on my bottom end from the hairbrush, I went into a crying, screaming fit and was trying my best to pull loose from her monstrous grip that she had on me. The whole time I climbed the staircase to the room upstairs, I cried out to her,

"I'm sorry, I didn't hurt him, I wasn't going to drop him, I just wanted something to play with, I don't have any toys," and she beat me with every step I climbed.

Once we made it to the top of the stairs and into the room, she grabbed me again, threw me to the floor, and pointed to some toys that were piled up in a corner of the room. She screamed,

"What are these, aren't these toys? There are plenty of toys here for you to play with." "Yes, but these are your toys. I didn't know that I could play with them. I didn't even know they were here," I cried out to her. Then she grabbed a toy, threw it at me, and yelled, "And you better not come down these stairs until I say you can come down, do you hear me you little brat?" Well believe me, going back down those stairs was the last thing I wanted to do anyway!

After she left the room and went back down stairs, I stood there for a minute stunned at what had just happen. I couldn't believe I had been beaten over picking up her dog. From that moment on I knew I would need to always be on my best behavior, especially around her.

After I regained my composure I began to examine my body to see what kind of marks she had left on me. When I looked at my bottom end, I saw bruises and long scratch marks with blood oozing out of them. There wasn't a bathroom upstairs for me to go wash the blood off my bottom, so I had no choice but to bleed on to my under clothes.

After a period of time had gone by, the foster mom came to the bottom of the staircase and yelled up to me, "Sandy, you can come down stairs now, it's time to eat supper." I always dreaded supper time at their house because she would cook food that I had never had before, neither with my parents nor in previous foster homes. Also, I would easily get sick at my stomach while eating due to lack of food when I lived with my parents.

When I came back down stairs from being left in the upstairs room, for who knows how long, the foster dad had come home from work by that time. The foster mom was so pleased with the beating she had given me that she told her husband what a terrible brat I had been that day and how she needed to give me a beating. Then with a hateful tone she said, "Go over to your dad, Sandy, and let him see what I did to you today". Again, I was shocked at what she had just commanded me to do, I was a shy little girl, and it embarrassed me so much to have to pull my pants down in front of this man so he could look at my bottom.

After the foster dad looked at my bottom he then commented, "Well I guess you will be good tomorrow, won't you?" We all went and sat down at the dining room table to eat supper. As I tried to eat what she had cooked, I could feel my stomach churning inside and knew I wouldn't be able to eat what she had prepared. My stomach just could not handle the spicy foods that she always cooked, and so like many nights before, I was made to sit at the table until I either ate the food or it was time to go to bed.

I recall one night at supper time she had cooked sauerkraut and polish sausage. Not wanting to make her mad, I tried my best to eat it, but just the smell alone was making me sick. "This is what we eat at this house and you better get used to it," she snapped at me. Needless to say I spent another night sitting at the dinner table until bedtime.

The next evening for supper I couldn't believe it but she had sauerkraut and polish sausage again. When I saw what we were having, I just chalked it up to here goes another night of sitting at the table alone until bedtime. As soon as we all sat down to eat, she said, "Sandy, I have cooked this food and, little girl, you're going to eat it if I have to shove it down your throat." She meant every word she said because when I didn't pick up my fork to eat, she jumped up out of her chair, came over to where I sat and grabbed a handful of my hair. She then jerked my head back, picked up my fork with sauerkraut piled on top and shoved it down my throat.

Instantly the pain from the fork, the smell and taste of the food made me throw up. This enraged her even more; that I had thrown up at the table and so then she yelled at me, *Now you eat that!* I sat there crying and said, "I can't, there is throw-up in my bowl!" "Here is a spoon and you just eat it anyway" she screamed.

I was so sick to my stomach, but terrified of what she was going to do to me next, so I picked up the spoon and attempted to *eat my own vomit.* Within seconds of putting the spoon in my mouth, I threw up again. *"I'm sorry, I'm sorry,"* I cried as I sat there *covered in vomit.* Then I was jerked out of my chair by the hair of my head and drug on the floor to the toilet in the bathroom where I throw up again. "If you're going to throw up, this is where you throw up," she screamed at me as she was dunking my head in the toilet and my mouth and nose sucked in the vomit. As I raised my head up out of the toilet, it just kept running through my mind that this is where people go to the bathroom, and so I threw up again. She then dunked my head back down in the toilet with the vomit and screamed at me, "This better be where you throw up from now on, do you understand!"

What happen to me after that last head dunking was a blur to my memory, but I do plainly remember, when going to bed that night, *I talked to the invisible God that I had been told about in the previous foster home.* I still wasn't quite sure of who or what he was, but at that moment He was all I had to turn to for help. I laid in my bed terrified, knowing the next time that the foster mom got her hands on me she just might kill me so I said,

"God I am just a little girl, please take care of me until I am big enough to take care of myself."

If beatings and forced to eat vomit weren't enough to endure by the foster mom, then my next nightmare to live through was *being abused* by the foster mom's brother, who shared a bedroom with me. There were bunk beds in our room; the top bed was mine and he slept on the bottom bed. I was asleep in my bed when he had come home from drinking at the bar one night. I remember being awakened by someone's hand touching me. When I opened my eyes I saw him standing near my face. Startled! I sat straight up in the bed and said, "What are you doing, what do you want?" I was so scared! What's he going to do to me, I thought to myself. At that moment my mind began to drift back to when my mother's boyfriend, Fred, would come in the night to our bedroom. I wondered if he would do the same things to me that Fred did. Of course I wanted no part of that and told him to please leave me alone. But once again, I would be abused. He had his mind set on what he was going to do with me and nothing I said or did was going to change it.

I'm terrified out of my mind by this point and totally clueless as to what is happening. His forceful hands continued to hold me as I struggled to pull away from him. At that very moment, I wanted desperately for someone to come save me from this BAD MAN but I knew I was all alone and no one was going to come and rescue me.

I then remembered about God, so once again I began to ask God to help me survive this night. God heard me and the BAD MAN stopped. And then he said, "You better not tell anyone about this because I will hurt you if you do."

As I laid in my bed afterward, I thought to myself, it's over, I'm okay, I lived through it. Little did I know though, that night was just the start of many more just like it to come. Every night at bed time I would lie in bed and cry, hoping he would not come home. When I would hear the front door open I would quickly dry my tears and pretend to be asleep, but that didn't stop him. Between the beatings and being force fed from the foster mom during the day and being abused by her brother at night, I thought in my mind *that I would die in this home before anyone would save me.*

Then to my surprise, Ms. Brown, a different Social Worker that had been assigned to my case came to the home to see me. Apparently, there was an older girl that was also living in the home and the foster mother's brother had been trying to do the same thing to her. I was told years later that she would hear me crying at night and figured he was abusing me also. So without the foster mother's knowledge she found my Social Worker's phone number, called her, and told her that I was being abused.

When Ms. Brown arrived at the foster home, she told me her name and then said, "I'm your new Social Worker, Sandy, and I am here to check on you and make sure you're doing okay." Even though I had never met her before that day, I was so glad to see a friendly face. Ms. Brown then told the foster mother that she wanted to talk to me alone in my bedroom. Once were in my room, Ms. Brown closed the door and said, "Let's go sit on the bed, Sandy, and talk for a while." That was fine with me because I knew as long as Ms. Brown was there no one was going to hurt me.

After we sat down on the bottom bunk bed, Ms. Brown pulled out a rag doll from her purse and asked me if I would like to play with the doll while we talked. I had no dolls of my own, so I was more than happy to. While I was playing with the doll, Ms. Brown began to ask me questions about if anyone had ever touched me where they shouldn't, like on my private parts of my body. I wanted to speak up that very second and tell her everything that these people had done to me, but I was too afraid to answer her. I knew if I told her anything the foster mom would beat me after Ms. Brown left.

Ms. Brown, sensing my fear, said, "Sandy, if someone has touched you, can you point to that body part on the doll" I pointed to the spot on the doll like she asked me to. Ms. Brown then asked me to tell her about what had happened. I started to cry and told her I couldn't, because even though the door was shut, I was still afraid the foster mom would hear me and then I would get in trouble. Ms. Brown said, "You can whisper in my ear if you want to Sandy." But even whispering in her ear was not enough for me. That foster family had abused me so severely that *I literally was in fear for my life.* I then told Ms. Brown that we had to go to the corner of the bedroom, sit on the floor with me on her lap and then I would whisper in her ear all the things they had done to me.

Once I felt safe in the corner of the room with Ms. Brown, the flood gates opened up to the river of tears that I had been holding back. I sobbed my heart out as I sat on her lap and cupped my hands around her ear and whispered to her all the *inhumane* things this foster family had done to me. When I was done she stood up and said she had to leave, but would come back for me to take me to another foster home. Instantly I went into a state of panic! I wrapped my arms around her waist, begged and pleaded for her not to leave me. They will know I told you and will beat me," I cried to her. Ms. Brown then pried my arms loose from her waist, knelt down beside me and said, "Sandy, I promise you, these people will not lay a hand on you again! I promise I will be back soon to get you, so you stay in this room and lock the door behind me until I come back for you, okay?" I agreed to do as she said and when she left I quickly locked the door.

I don't remember how much time had gone by before she came back for me, but I do remember the foster mother sitting in a chair at the dinner table when I came out of my room. Ms. Brown was holding my hand and we were going to the door to leave when the foster mother held out her arms for me to go to her. I really didn't want to, but Ms. Brown said, "It's okay, Sandy, you can go over to her and see what she wants. The foster mother then picked me up, set me down on her lap and began to tell me how sorry she was, that she didn't know what her brother was doing to me. I think I could have accepted that apology had she not been abusing me herself. I did find out years later that this foster home was shut down and the foster mother's brother did go to jail for what he had done to me.

Forth Foster Home:

Upon arriving at this home, I was very nervous as Ms. Brown and I stood waiting for the front door to open. Although Ms. Brown had told me that this would be a really nice foster home for me to live in, I had heard that same statement before, so I was still apprehensive about being left alone there. Once again I had no way of knowing what kind of people lived here. Would they be nice or would they be abusive, I wondered.

An elderly lady opened the door and with a warm smile she invited Ms. Brown and me to come in. She introduced herself to me as Fay, and then said, "But if you would like to call me mama, that would be okay too." We all sat down in the living room while Ms. Brown brought Florence up to date about my past. When it was time for Ms. Brown to leave, for the first time while in foster care, I was not afraid to be left at a foster home with strangers.

Fay had two daughters of her own, although I only met one. It was years later when I would find out that her other daughter had died from a heart condition. I have nothing but fond memories of this foster home. Fay was a very kind and loving person and she became to me the mama I so desperately needed.

Fay lived in a neighborhood that had other children for me to play with. Unlike the previous foster home where I was not allowed outside, if the weather was good, Fay would allow me to go play with my new friends. I was starting to be a little girl again, concerning myself with friends and toys, instead of worrying from one minute to the next if I was going to be beaten or killed.

I started Kindergarten while living with Fay and I really enjoyed going to school, to be with my friends there also. One day after I arrived home from school, Fay called me into the kitchen and said she needed to talk to me. She began telling me about how long I had been in foster care and that the State was going to allow me to be adopted. After she explained to me what being adopted meant, I then said, "I want you to be my forever mama, can you adopt me?" I loved Fay with all my heart and I never wanted to leave her! She was very good to me and the thought of being taken from her just broke my heart.

With tears in her eyes, Fay said, "I love you to, Sandy, and would love to adopt you, but the State won't let me because I'm too old." "You're not too old for me," I replied back as I began to cry. Then Fay picked me up, sat me down on the kitchen table, and held me in her arms while I cried and begged her not to let the State take me away from her.

A few days had passed by when Fay came to me again, only this time to tell me what I had been dreading to hear. "The State had found a couple that was considering adopting you Sandy and they have a little boy and girl about the same age as you. Isn't that good news?," Fay said to me. I really had mixed feelings about the whole adopting thing, because I loved Fay and didn't want to leave her, yet on the other hand, having a forever family again sounded good also. "When do I have to leave?," I asked Fay. Fay replied, "When school lets out for summer break, Sandy, and don't worry honey, because it's just a trial visit anyway. Fay could tell I didn't understand what a trial visit meant, so she explained to me that going to their house just for the summer would give this family time to see if they wanted to adopt me and it would also give me some time to see if I wanted them to be my new mom and dad. Knowing it was just a trial visit and not a permanent move with this family, I was okay with going, plus having a brother and sister to play with again sounded pretty good too.

Summer break had arrived and it was time for me to go on my trial visit. Like each time before when I would go to a new home, I was nervous and wondering if they would be nice parents or mean parents. I also wondered if their children would like me or would they be mean to me. Upon arriving at their home, the mom and dad greeted me with warm smiles and hugs and the little girl and boy were very friendly as well. I only visited with this family for one month, so due to the short period of time I was with them, I have few memories. Although I do remember that the whole family welcomed me in their home and were very nice to me throughout my visit with them. I also have a vague memory of laughing and playing with their little boy and girl on a swing set and in their swimming pool in the backyard.

When my visit was over the foster parents took me back to Fay's house. Before leaving they stated to Fay that they would let her know their decision on adopting me within a couple of weeks. Of course deep down inside I was hoping they wouldn't want to because I didn't want to leave Fay. During those next couple of weeks Fay and I stayed busy with shopping for school clothes and supplies. Summer break had come to an end and school was ready to start back.

Not long after I had started first grade, Fay received a phone call from the couple I had visited with over the summer. They stated to her that after serious consideration they had decided not to adopt me. They explained to Fay that after discussing their wanting to adopt me with their two children, they felt that their children were jealous of the attention shown to me, and felt adopting me would cause friction in their family. When Fay gave me the news the couple had decided not to adopt me, I was so happy! I ran over to Fay, wrapped my arms around her waist, hugged her and said, "I'm so glad mama, now I can stay with you." Fay hugged me back and told me how much she loved me, but that the State would begin looking for another adoptive home for me. I knew she was right, but I decided to not think about being adopted and I would just enjoy what time I had left, to live with Fay.

CHAPTER SIX

MEETING MY ADOPTIVE FAMILY

The events that take place next are ones that I distinctly remember because my life, as I knew it, was about to change again and this time *my Identity and name would be forever taken from me!*

I was six years old by this time and in kindergarten. As I think back to that time in my life, it is so vivid in my mind as if it was yesterday when this happened. Having your identity taken from you is mentally and emotionally traumatising. It seemed the harder I tried to hold on to the person I was. The more my new family and friends wanted to erase the memories of my past. They would make me feel that *being Sandy, the person I was born to be, was damaged goods*. In other words, they wanted me to believe that the first five years of my life never happened.

It was in the middle of the first semester of school and I was outside having fun, playing with my friends and just being a little girl. Fay came to the door and called me to come into the house because she wanted to talk to me about something. I said okay, and ran in the house to see what she wanted. Once inside Fay told me to sit down at the kitchen table because she had something to tell me. "There is another couple that might be interested in adopting you Sandy. Isn't that wonderful?," Fay said.

In that moment my thoughts went from being that happy little girl who was just outside playing, to being the scared, insecure and homeless child I had been so many times before.

I asked if she knew the couple, and she said, "Yes, I know the woman because she's the lady who styles my hair. I haven't met her husband yet, but her name is Ms. Joni. She's a beautician and has her own beauty shop. She's really a nice lady Sandy, and I think you will like her," said Fay. At that time I still had mixed feelings about being adopted and having to leave Fay, but I was also tired of my class mates at school teasing me for being a foster child. They would say, *"Ha, no one wants you, Sandy. Your own parents didn't even want you because they gave you away!"* It's hard to find the words to express how much this affected me. I was deeply hurt and even though it was children who were saying these things to me, their cruel words would haunt me for many years to come. I thought to myself if I'm adopted the kids at school won't be able to make fun of me anymore, because then I will have a family with a mom and dad just like they do. So being adopted actually sounded pretty good to me. "Sandy, what do you think about going with me the next time I have my hair styled? This way you and Ms. Joni can meet each other," Fay asked. I told her that would be okay and then asked if I could go back outside to play.

The day came when it was time to meet my perspective new mother. My nerves had kicked in as usual. I could feel my heart racing and it seemed a million thoughts were running through my mind. "Will Ms. Joni really be a nice person? I wonder what she looks like and I wonder if she will like me. I hope her husband isn't mean," I was thinking to myself.

While on the drive to Ms. Joni's Beauty Salon, Fay spoke to me on how to behave and to remember my manners. I assured her I would remember and then Fay said, "Now, Sandy, when we get to the Beauty Salon, I will point Ms. Joni out to you, then you run up to her with a big smile, hug her around the waist, and tell her your name." "Maybe she won't like me doing that and will get mad at me," I replied. Then Fay reassured me that Ms. Joni loved children and really wanted a little girl of her own.

When we arrived at the Beauty Salon I did exactly as Fay had instructed. After Fay pointed Ms. Joni out to me, I ran straight to her. I said, Hi Ms. Joni," hugged her waist and said, My name is Sandy." To my surprise, with a big smile and a laugh in her voice she said, "Well, hello there, Sandy, you sure are a pretty little girl. I have been so anxious to meet you and honey you can just call me Aunt Joni." I was happy to call her Aunt Joni because it made me feel like I was already a part of her family.

After my first meeting with Aunt Joni she and Fay scheduled a weekend during my school break for me to meet her husband and son. Upon arriving at their home I was greeted with warm smiles and hugs. We all went into the living room and Aunt Joni introduced me to her husband, Dick, and her ten year old son, Roy. The first thing I asked Aunt Joni was, "Do I call your husband Uncle Dick?" Aunt Joni laughed and replied, "Yes, Sandy, that's a good idea. You just call him Uncle Dick. At first I was a little leery of getting too close to Uncle Dick due to the abuse that I had already gone through. I was very afraid of men, but after sitting on his lap and talking with him, I thought he was really nice too. I wasn't really sure how I felt about their son Roy. I mean, he seemed nice enough but when I thought back to times spent with my brother John, I remembered how mean brothers could sometimes be. I also remembered, though, how much I missed my siblings and thought it would be nice to have someone to play with again. So I decided if Roy was nice to me I would be nice to him and except him as my brother if I was adopted.

That weekend Uncle Dick and Aunt Joni took me to meet some of their family members and a few of their friends. Aunt Joni knew that as a foster child, I had very few clothes or toys of my own, so they also took me shopping and bought me clothes and toys to play with. I remember being so excited going from one store to another. As we would walk by what I thought was beautiful, colorful dresses that sparkled in clothing stores I would run and touch each one. I had never seen clothes that looked like that before so I was totally amazed at what I was seeing. Then when we went into the toy store I was beside myself with excitement. I had never seen so many different toys to play with and of course I wanted every toy on the shelf. Aunt Joni told me I could pick one thing out and she would buy it for me, so because I had only had one doll that I could remember, I chose a doll. Although I think she felt sorry for me and did buy me a couple more toys.

I remember being so appreciative and thanking her several times for the toys and clothes she had bought me. At six years old, I knew what it was like to have nothing and to be mistreated. So I was always very thankful for anything that was given to me. I was also very thankful for anyone who was good to me and didn't abuse me. Because Aunt Joni and Uncle Dick were good to me and treated me like a human being and not someone's throwaway child to be used and abused. They won my heart which allowed me to let go of the strong bond I had with Fay. I still loved Fay deeply, but I was now able to move on to another chapter in my book of life. I was happy they were going to adopt me and was excited to be starting my life over, so to speak, with a new family.

I went every weekend to visit them. When school was over for summer break, I then moved in with Uncle Dick and Aunt Joni permanently. I remember the day I moved in with them being very emotional for me. I was happy about finally getting to live with them, but I was also very sad to leave Fay. Through all the foster homes I had lived in, Fay had been the only one that was truly a mother to me. I knew I would miss her very much and cried when I had to tell her good bye. I asked her if she would come visit me sometime and with tears in her eyes she said, "Of course I will Sandy, I promise." With that said, I left Fay's home broken hearted, but at the same time eager and happy to start my new life.

CHAPTER SEVEN

ADOPTION AND NAME CHANGE

I had just completed kindergarten when I went to live with my adoptive family. Uncle Dick, Aunt Joni and their son Roy accepted me into their home with love and treated me as if I had lived with them from the time of my birth. I felt as if the weight of the whole world had been lifted off my shoulders. *After two torturous years of severe abuse, neglect, fear of death and loneliness, I once again had a home and family I could call my own.*

After arriving at their home, Aunt Joni and I went into my new bedroom and began to unpack the few worldly possessions I had brought with me. With excitement we laughed and talked while sorting through my things and putting them neatly away. As we talked Aunt Joni said to me, "Sandy, now that you are living with us and we are going to adopt you, you can call us mom and dad." it really felt wonderful having forever parents again, so I was happy to call them my mom and dad. I replied, "Okay mom", as I giggled with joy.

As time passed by, I adjusted and settled into my new family's routine and way of life. I once again was a happy little girl, concerning myself only with what friend or toy I would play with next. During this time, my mom came to me and said that she wanted to talk to me. She began by telling me that she and my dad had also adopted Roy. She explained to me how his adoption came about and how he was only three days old when they brought him home from the hospital. Finding out that Roy was adopted made me feel better about my own adoption. I felt, if nothing else, he and I at least had that much in common.

She then told me that even though I now belonged to them, it was going to take two years before my adoption would be final. She explained the reason for the two year waiting period was to give Gene, my biological mother, time to come back for me if she wanted to. By this time in my life, I had built up anger and resentment toward Gene. *I felt like she had just thrown me away like a piece of trash. I totally blamed her for the two years of abuse I had suffered and lived through.* So hearing this really concerned me because going back to live with Gene was the last thing I wanted to do. Seeing my facial expression filled with worry and fear, my mom said, "Don't worry Sandy. Gene moved out of state and I'm pretty sure she won't be coming back." "How do you know she won't come back?," I asked. "Because, if Gene comes back to Michigan, she can be arrested for child abandonment," Mom said. Knowing Gene had moved eased my mind somewhat but it still bothered me to know she had that right.

As time went on I tried not to think about Gene and just enjoyed the family I had grown to trust and love. I had started a new school, made new friends, and played and had disagreements with my brother Roy, as all siblings do. My life was finally, for the most part, normal, aside from the *occasional nightmares of past abuse.* We would go on family vacations, which would allow me to meet more of their friends and family members. I was going places and doing things that I had never done before. I was now happy once again and content with my new life.

My mom had one sibling, a sister named Patricia that lives in Ohio. One of our vacation trips was to Ohio so I could meet Aunt Patricia, her husband Uncle Ben, and their three boys. They were all very loving and kind to me and instantly accepted me as part of their family. Through the years, I grew to love them all dearly and to this day I still consider them my family.

Before I knew it the two year waiting period had passed by and the day to finalize my adoption had arrived. I was eight years old by this time and very much aware of what being adopted would mean for me and the rest of my life. Before this day had arrived, my mom told me that I would be allowed to change my name if I wanted to. Even though I was happy with my new life, I still had deep anger and resentment toward Gene. I wanted nothing from her, which included the name she had given me from birth. I told my mom that I wanted to change my name to her name Joni. She laughed and thanked me for wanting her name, but said I should pick another name. She explained that both of us being called by the same name would be too confusing for my dad, Roy, and everyone else that knew us. When I thought about what she said I agreed with her. I then thought of my Aunt Patricia, my mom's sister. I thought about how much I loved Aunt Patricia and how I really liked her name. My mom seemed really delighted that I had chosen her sister's name and said okay. We both agreed that my new name then would be Patsy Jo. She then said Patti could be my nick name. I was happy to have this name and be called Patti, because then I would be named after both my Aunt and my mom, the two women in my life that I loved and respected the most.

I knew the adoption would change my life again in some ways because now I would be legally their daughter. Also having a new name would take getting used to, not just for me, but for everyone that knew me, especially my friends at school. My mom then told me that I would have to talk to the judge in his chambers. She explained to me that the judge would want to know my feelings about being adopted. She said he would also want to know if I was in agreement with having my name changed. I was excited to know that my adoption would now be final, but I was also afraid to talk to the judge.

After arriving at the court house the day of my adoption, my mom, dad and I all sat down on a bench that was facing the judge's chambers. While sitting on the bench waiting to be called into the judge's office, I could feel myself getting really nervous and scared. I remember looking up at my mom and telling her how scared I was and that I didn't want to talk to the judge. She told me not to worry or to be afraid that, everything would be okay, and that the judge would be nice to me. I felt somewhat better hearing what she said, but I was still very anxious for the whole thing to be over.

Inside the judge's chambers were three chairs that were in front of his desk. We each one sat down and waited for the judge to begin our meeting. Like my mom had told me, the judge asked me all the questions she said he would. The judge was a very nice man and seemed to be concerned for my wellbeing. After granting the adoption, the judge ended the meeting with a hand shake to all of us. He then wished us a happy life together as a family. Upon leaving the judge's chambers I felt instant relief. The adoption being final meant that I didn't have to worry anymore about going to another abusive foster home. It also meant that Geneva would not be allowed to come back for me. To celebrate this special occasion, after leaving the court house, the three of us went to a restaurant for lunch.

One would now think that my adoption and having a permanent home and family would mean no more abuse. For me that wasn't the case, because there would still be more abuse to come.

CHAPTER EIGHT

ABUSE AFTER ADOPTION

It wasn't long after my adoption, things at home slowly began to change. I started noticing that my mom and dad were having a lot of arguments. Most of their arguments were over my dad's hobby which was gambling. I soon realized that my parent's marital problems had started long before I had come into their life.

My dad's hobby had been kept hidden from Fay, me, and my Social Worker, during the two year waiting period, before my adoption. At first their fighting would make me cry because it would scare me. I wasn't use to adults fighting, so I didn't know what to expect. I would hide in my bedroom and not come out until they stopped yelling at each other. It seemed after a while my dad's compulsion with his hobby became more frequent and so did their fighting. When I realized that they weren't going to kill each other, or me while fighting, I was able to overcome my fear. Although I wasn't afraid anymore, it did seriously affect me mentally and emotionally. I was very attached to my mom, so I felt bad for her, and understood why she would get so upset with him. On the other hand, I loved my dad too, and felt just as bad for him. It seemed I was always on edge never knowing when the next fight was going to start. Many times when my parents argued, Roy and I would be put in the middle, and I would feel like we were being forced to choose sides.

We always knew when my dad came home from gambling whether he won or lost money. If he won, he would always be in a good mood and bring pizza or donuts home for us to eat. Being young kids Roy and I were always happy the nights he won and would eagerly eat the food that he would bring. If my dad lost his pay check he would come home empty handed, in a bad mood, and would snap at Roy and me over the smallest things. Of course this would make my mom angry and then the colorful vocabulary and name calling would start between the two of them. Sometimes I would get so tired of hearing them fight, I would open my bedroom door and yell out to them, "Please stop fighting!" Sometimes it worked and they would actually stop, but most times I was ignored and the fighting would continue.

Just when I thought my parent's fighting would be the worst thing that I would have to endure while living at home, I was in for a big surprise. This time, the fighting would be with me, and my brother Roy. He was twelve years old and I was eight when it started.

I remember plainly the first argument we had. It was sometime in the middle of the night after my parents had gone to bed and I had fallen asleep. I was awaken by the sound of foot steps in my room. It terrified me at first because I thought a burglar had come in our home and was trying to hurt me. I quickly sat up in the bed and looked to see who was in my room. When I saw Roy sitting on the floor beside my bed, I was in complete shock. I couldn't believe what my eyes were seeing. I was so angry with him I yelled at him to go back to his own room. He said okay, and then left my bedroom.

He was my brother and only four years older than me so I wasn't afraid of him, but I was very upset with him for waking me up. He caused horrible memories from past abuse to come rushing back to my mind. Even at that time in my life I was still having nightmares from my past. Now my nightmares would just get worse.

The next morning when I got out of bed I went straight to my mom and told her what Roy had done in the middle of the night. She was very upset with him. She harshly scolded him and said to him, "It better not happen again." Roy assured her that it wouldn't. Two nights went by without him coming into my room so I thought my mom's scolding had worked, but I was wrong. On the third night I was awakened again by Roy. Again, in anger, I yell at him and told him that I was going to tell mom. He gets up off the floor and said, "You better not," as he left my room. I laid there in bed very upset over what he was doing. I had thought being mistreated was over for me once my parents had adopted me. *I never dreamed I would live through it again with this family.*

When I got up the next morning I went to my mom again. I told her that Roy had come back in my room in the middle of the night. She got mad, but this time at me also. She said, "I have had just about enough of this crap, and I'm telling both of you it better stop." I was shocked! I couldn't believe I was getting yelled at also. Her getting mad at me, too, just opened the door for Roy, because then he knew I wouldn't tell on him anymore.

Just when I thought the problem with Roy had been resolved, it started up again. This time because my mom allowed him to babysit me when she and my dad would go out. After they would leave the house, like most kids do, I would run through the house and jump up and down on the furniture. The first time that he was babysitting me I was jumping on our sofa in the living room and when I sat down, he touched me. The first time, I really didn't think much about it. I thought he had just got in my way by accident. Then I started noticing that each time I would sit down, his hand would always be to where he could grab me. He would laugh and tell me to see how high I could jump. When I figured out what he was doing, I stopped jumping on the sofa and began playing on the floor. Even then he would find a reason to get on the floor with me. It seemed no matter where I played he was always there.

I knew if I told my mom she wouldn't do anything to Roy and I would just get yelled at for telling her. So of course I dreaded each time that my parents would go out and leave him to babysit me. But as time went on, I grew older, and learned how to avoid him. Eventually he stopped bothering me but I wasn't able to feel in my heart that brother and sister bond anymore. He now was just someone I lived with who happened to have the same parents I did. For a long time, I even guarded my feelings towards my mom. For the life of me, I just couldn't understand why she reacted the way she did when she found out what Roy was doing to me. As time passed though, the three of us somehow were able to put this problem behind us, and go on with our life.

For the next two years, our lives were like your average suburban family in a crime filled city. My dad worked on the on the west side of the city. My mom moved her beauty shop into our basement so she could be at home with Roy and me. I enjoyed her being home with us and I would spend a lot of my time in the basement playing and talking with her customers. Although my parents still had their arguments, the fighting had become less frequent. On Sundays we went to church and sometimes we would go visit my parents' friends afterward. The Sundays we didn't go visiting, my mom would always cook a big Sunday dinner. I actually started feeling that maybe my life was going to be okay after all.

I was about eleven years old by this time and Roy and I both were going to have to change schools. This really concerned my parents because some of the schools had been rioting during that time. My parents felt the crime in the city was too much and wanted to move away from it. My mom had an aunt and uncle who lived in Mississippi. Her aunt's name was Rose and mom was very close to her. My mom told Aunt Rose about how bad things were getting in Michigan and how she and my dad were wanting to move. Aunt Rose told my mom about a country grocery store that was for sale and that they should come and look at it. School was letting out for summer break at that time so we all went to Mississippi for a visit.

This was my first time to meet Aunt Rose and Uncle Mike. They were very nice to me and I really enjoyed our visit with them. After a couple of days of visiting and seeing the sights, Aunt Rose took us to see the store that was for sale. I must have been born country, because I fell in love with the store and the small little community it was in. I was so hoping that my parents would buy the store and move our family to the country. I made sure to tell them how much I liked it and wanted us to move there.

December 30, 1971, my wish came true. My parents bought the store and we were moving to Mississippi. January 1, 1972, was my family's first day of being the proud new owners of this little country store. I had lived in a big city since birth, so living in the country now was like culture shock. Suddenly, my life was now one big adventure. I was learning about different animals that I had only seen in a zoo before. Also to fit in and make friends at school, I had to learn the southern way of life.

My parents enrolled Roy and me in a private school that was within walking distance of our store. At first, it was hard for me to make friends. Once my class mates found out I was from the north they didn't want anything to do with me. They would pick on me and say go home Yankee, we don't want you here. Of course this would deeply hurt my feelings and many times I would go home from school crying. But, as always, time had a way of changing things and eventually they forgot about me coming from the north and accepted me as one of them.

Our store was located in what was considered a resort area. Just a few miles past our store was a large dam that was longer than your eyes could see. Below the dam was a spillway surrounded by a large camp ground. People from everywhere would come there to camp out, fish, and go swimming at the beach. This was also considered a good area for hunting as well.

Our store was stocked with everything a vacationer needed for camping and fishing. We had cabins for rent, a bait shop filled with a large variety of bait, and fishing supplies, boats for rent and much more. The store stayed busy most times and there was always plenty of work to be done. After school, Roy and I were expected to help out in the store by waiting on customers or stocking the shelves. The store sat on five acres of land so when business was slow, I was allowed to leave the store and go exploring on our property. I ran and played through the fields and enjoyed every second of the beauty and peacefulness I saw and felt from living in the country.

Before I knew it, a year had gone by and I was now thirteen years old. I had somehow learned to live with the deep hidden scars from past abuse and had become an inquisitive little girl who was growing into young womanhood. I was hungry for knowledge of the world and everything it had to offer. I was determined that I would not let my severe abusive childhood prevent or hinder me from having a meaningful and productive life. I loved going to school and always tried my best to make good grades. My dreams and goals were to go to college, have a career, and maybe even become a doctor someday. I would then get married and have a family of my own. It seemed like I had the next several years of my life all planed out and my being abused days were finally over. At least so I thought.

By this point my dad's hobby was now football games or playing cards. On Sundays, during football season, when the store was slow, he would walk to our house which was only a few hundred feet from the store and watch the games on TV. Roy really didn't care much about sports and was more into being a mechanic and fixing up old cars. On the other hand, I was on the basketball and track team in school so my dad, knowing how much I liked sports, and enjoyed the thrill of competition, would always ask me which football team did I think was going to win. I knew nothing about professional football but to make my dad happy I would always choose a team.

One Sunday, before going to the house to watch the football game, my dad asked me if I wanted to go with him. The newness and excitement of having the store had worn off by this time, so I jumped at the chance to get a break from working in it. We each took a soda and snack from the store and walked to the house. When we got there, my dad turned the TV on and we both sat down on the sofa to watch the game. I really didn't care anything about watching the game, but I did enjoy the time spent with my dad.

The following Sunday, once again, my dad and I were sitting on the sofa watching the football game. Out of the clear blue he reaches over, grabs me and said jokingly, "Boy, Patti, I can tell your really starting to grow up now." *I was floored, flabbergasted, stunned and then some!* I couldn't believe the man I had completely trusted, grown to love, and called my dad had just put his hands on me. My feelings were hurt and my heart was crushed. At that moment, I knew even though I had felt like his daughter, to him I was nothing more than just someone he had helped raise. In my heart and mind, I had just lost another father. Instantly I told him to stop and scooted away from him on the sofa. The whole time I thought, I can't believe this is happening to me again! He then scooted closer to me and grabbed me again. This time I told him, "If you don't stop, I'm telling mom." With a laugh he said, "You better not or I will spank you." I didn't really think he would spank me, but I also didn't want to cause problems in the family either, so I decided not to tell my mom at this time.

The following Sunday, when it was time for the game to start my dad said, "Come on Patti, let's go watch the game." Naturally I didn't want to go, so I told him that I wanted to stay with my mom in the store. He said, "No, I want you to go with me, because you being there brings me good luck." Of course, I didn't believe that for one second, but I could tell by the tone of his voice that I had to go with him. I was afraid of my dad; he could have a violent temper if provoked. I knew this, because I had already witnessed him hit my mom in past arguments.

Once we made it in the house he insisted that I had to sit on the sofa next to him. I did as I was told, praying the whole time that he wouldn't put his hands on me. During half time he looked over at me and grabbed me. With an angry tone I jumped up, yelled at him to stop, and went back to the store. I was so mad at him and still couldn't believe what he was doing to me. *In my mind it was his place to protect me, not abuse me.* I wanted to tell my mom right then, but decided to wait till she and I were alone.

The next night, after the store closed, my mom and I had gone to the house and were sitting in the kitchen alone. Roy was away in college and my dad had gone to play cards with his friends in the city which was fifteen miles from where we lived. My dad always came home late when he was out playing cards, so I knew this would be a good time to tell my mom about what he was doing to me. As my mom and I were talking, I began to tell her all the things my dad had done and said to me. As she questioned me about the things he did, and the times that it happen, I could see the rage building inside her. She said a few choice words and then started to cry. When I saw how upset she was I felt bad about telling her and I too began to cry. I begged her to wait till I was at school before she said anything to him and she promised me she would.

The next day when I came home from school I knew she had told my dad about our conversation the night before. I could feel the tension and anger between them the minute I walked in the store. Later that night, as I laid in my bed, I could hear them screaming and swearing at each other as loud as they could. At this point I was a complete wreck myself. It seemed once again, my life was unstable and I was unsure of my future. The next day my mom told me not to worry and said that my dad wouldn't be abusing me anymore. Although in my mind the damage had been done and I knew his and my relationship would never be the same again.

Another year had passed and I was now fourteen. It seemed that hardly a day would go by that my parents weren't at each other's throats. Night after night, I would lay in bed listening to them screaming at each other over my dad's new hobbies. At times, their anger would get so out of control that it would even escalate to physical violence. This would always frighten me because I was afraid my dad would go too far and seriously hurt my mom. The constant fighting between my parents made it nearly impossible for me to concentrate at school or study at home.

One morning during this time, my dad had slept in and my mom had left the house to open the store. I was just about to leave the house myself to go and help her when my dad called me to come in his room. He then told me to come closer to the bed because he wanted me to do something for him. Of course, instantly I said no and turned around to leave the room. In a mean forceful voice he said, "You better do as I say and get over here right now." Knowing how violent my dad's temper could get, and seeing the look on his face, I was too afraid not to do as he demanded. My mind drifted back and pictures of past abuse filled my mind. As I thought back to those times in my life, I could feel the anger raging inside me.

I told him that I was going to tell my mom what he had made me do. Jokingly he said, "I don't care, tell, I'm not afraid of your mom." Believe me, the first chance I got I told my mom everything that had happen, and also what my dad had said. I just knew she would be furious. I despised him now; I wanted her to divorce him. I mean by this time, I had lost all respect for him not only as my dad, but also as a man. Surprisingly though, when I told my mom, it seemed her anger was directed straight at me. She harshly snapped at me and said, "Well, Patti, if you didn't run around here with those skimpy shorts that you wear, maybe this wouldn't have happen!"

I COULD NOT BELIEVE MY EARS!! My mom, the woman I had grown to love and respect, had turned her back on me. I was having a hard enough time being a teenager and coping with puberty. I sure didn't need or want the added burden of a screwed up home life and parents that mistreated me. My attitude, goals and dreams had now changed. Instead of enjoying school, and thinking of college and a career, my mind focused once again on survival. I now knew that I was all alone in this world, and no one was going to save or protect me. From this time forward, all of our lives would drastically change.

My parents fought daily now. If they weren't arguing over my dad spending money, it was over the abuse my dad had done to me. I now had severe anger issues and had become a rebelling teenager with a serious attitude problem. I was fourteen, desperate, scared, and had lost all respect for both my parents. All I wanted or could think about was getting away from their abuse. Then like the flip of a light switch, I suddenly knew what I had to do. I would just have to run away.

The town I lived in, was a very small close knit community. Everyone knew their neighbor and everything about them. There were no secrets kept. Your personal affairs were common knowledge throughout the community. Because my parents owned one of only two grocery stores in this town, even the police knew my parents. I remember many times the police coming to our store just to visit and talk with my dad.

I ended up running away from home twice in that year. Both times I ran, the police found me, and took me back home. The second time I ran away, before I was allowed to get out of the police car, I first had to sit through a lecture from the police officer who picked me up. He told me what good people my parents were and how wrong I was for running away. He then went on to say how grateful I should be because he knew my parents, and that was the only reason he didn't take me to juvenile detention. I replied back to the officer, "My parents are mean to me, so take me to juvenile detention. I would rather be there than to go back home." Of course he didn't take me, and again told me what great parents I had. Then he continued to harshly scold me for my attitude and running away from home. I didn't tell the police officer about the abuse because I was too afraid that he wouldn't believe me. I also questioned in my mind, if the officer did believe me, what would happen to me next. So because of the uncertainty of what my future held for me, I kept the horrible secret of abuse to myself. Even though I was fourteen, I was still just a scared little girl in a lot of ways. Telling anyone about the abuse, which included the police, was just simply out of the question.

Of course my running away and the police getting involved made life at home worse than ever. Both my parents vented their anger towards me, and my life became unbearable. The close bond and relationship that I had with my mom was now gone. She blamed me not just for the abuse my dad had done to me, but also for the problems it had caused in her marriage, instead of making sure I wasn't left alone with my dad so he wouldn't abuse me anymore. My mom would leave me at home with my dad many times while she would go into the city to go shopping or whatever it was that she would do. My anger and resentment towards them both kept growing stronger each time it would happen.

Shortly after I had run away from home the second time, my brother Roy had come home from college for summer break. I was fifteen now and had just started to date. One night, after getting home from a date, I went into the kitchen for something to drink. Both my parents had gone to bed and had told Roy to stay up until I made it home. Roy came in the kitchen where I was and grabbed me. I could tell by his demeanor, and the smell of his breath, that he had been drinking. Then he said to me, "Sandy, you know I love you, and have always wanted you for myself." Instantly, I pulled away from him while telling him that my name was no longer Sandy, and to take his hands off me. I then left him standing in the kitchen, went to my bed room, and shut the door. As I laid in bed that night, thinking about how crazy my whole family was, I knew then I would need to do whatever it took to get away from all of them. I also thought about how much I loved learning at school and wanted to go to college. I didn't want to walk away from the goals and dreams, I had made for myself, but felt I was being forced to.

Being fifteen, and still immature, my ability to logically reason my problems out was not very good to say the least. All the years of abuse had caused me to be very emotionally unstable and not capable of make good choices or decisions. I knew I was too young to get a job and support myself, so in my mind, I only had two options. The first option was; I could stay at home, finish school, be abused by my dad and brother, and cope with my mom's anger. The second option; I would find someone I knew I could love, and get married. I went for the second option, and met Gary, the father of my children.

While Gary and I were dating, I told him about the abuse that I was living in at home. He became very angry and said he wanted to get me out of that house and away from my abusive family. He also told me how much he loved me and then asked me to marry him. I too had fallen in love with him by this time, so I happily accepted his proposal of marriage. The next day Gary approached my mom and asked her for my hand in marriage. Without hesitation my mom quickly said no, and told Gary that I was too young for marriage. Although we both knew she was right, we also knew getting married was the only way out for me.

Not long after my mom had said no, I found out that I was pregnant with my first child. Gary and I both were scared and happy at the same time about the pregnancy. We wanted children but not until much later after we were married. I felt I was a baby getting ready to have a baby. That was okay though, because Gary and I knew we would love this child and give it everything we possibly could. I also knew, out of concern for their reputation in the community, my parents would now sign for me to get married.

When my dad found out I was pregnant he became extremely angry. He began screaming at me and said I would never amount to anything. He told me that I was no better than a slut and I would sleep with anything that wore pants. He then went on to tell my mom, while I was standing there, that I wasn't their flesh and blood and I was nothing but trouble. He demanded that she sign the paper, because he wasn't going to allow me to live there any longer.

Well, I'm sure you can imagine how deeply my feelings were hurt after everything my dad had said. I went in my bed room, laid across my bed, and cried myself to sleep. Later that night, Gary came to the house to ask my parents again if they would sign for us to get married. Of course my dad told Gary that he wasn't getting much and that I couldn't even boil water. Gary said that he didn't mind because he knew how to cook. I wanted to laugh, but with my dad's temper ready to explode at any given moment, I knew that would not be a smart thing to do. After my dad had plenty of bad things to say about me, he told Gary and me that he and my mom would sign for us to get married. He also let us know that he didn't want me living there anymore, and we were getting married whether we wanted to or not. Of course that wasn't a problem for us because getting me away from my family's abuse is what we wanted anyway.

Somehow, by the grace of God, my parents and I managed to live the next couple of months under the same roof before Gary and I got married. After fifteen years, I was finally free from being abused. *Although I paid a high price for this freedom*, in my mind it was worth it to not be abused by my family any longer.

CHAPTER NINE

LOSS OF MY FIRST CHILD

I was fifteen when mine and Gary's first child, a precious little girl, was born. Because I was so young and had a very small body frame, I wasn't able to carry the pregnancy full term. She was born premature in the eighth month of my pregnancy, on September 25, 1976, at 10:50 pm.

I had been in labor for eighteen hours and was completely exhausted by the time she was born. I didn't get to see her in the delivery room, so the nurse stopped by the nursery window when taking me to my room. I struggled to raise myself up off the bed so I could to see my daughter for the first time. I will never, as long as I am breathing, forget that moment. When I saw her I thought she was the most beautiful baby in the whole world. She only weighed four pounds and was so tiny and fragile. Right away I commented on how small she was and expressed my concern to my husband and the nurse. They both told me not to worry because she was doing really well.

I felt better knowing that although small, my baby was okay. By this time it was midnight and after getting into my hospital room, I went straight to sleep. The next morning I woke up happy and full of excitement. I was a mama now; God had blessed me with a daughter of my own. I could not have been happier than

I was at that moment. I wanted to hold my baby so I called the nurse and asked her to bring my daughter to me. A few minutes later the nurse came to my room and told me that my doctor wanted to talk to me first before bringing my daughter in. I didn't think anything of it and anxiously waited for him to come to my room.

When the Doctor came into my room, I quickly told him that I was not able to hold my baby the night before. I asked him if it would be okay for the nurse to bring her to me. With a concerned expression on his face, he proceeded to tell me that my daughter had developed a breathing problem. He then explained to me that because she was premature, her lungs had not fully developed and they were filling up with her own body fluid. I was beside myself with worry and asked him if she was going to be okay. He stated that her condition was stable and that they were doing everything they could for her.

After she had been born the night before, my husband had gone home to get some rest. Being upset and scared for my daughter, I immediately called my husband and other family members. I explained to them what the doctor had said and told them they needed to come to the hospital. Upon arriving at the hospital, my husband, mom, and other family members all gathered in my room so we could all pray for her.

About two hours passed, and the Doctor came back to my room to update my husband and me on our daughter's condition. He then told us that she had gone from stable to critical. Gary and I both felt so helpless and we desperately wanted to do something, anything, that would help our daughter. So we demanded that she be transferred to another hospital that was better equipped to handle her condition. After the doctor left my room, *I got on my knees in my bed, crying my heart out, and begged God not to take her from me. I asked him to take my mom, dad, husband, even my life, but not her life.*

Another hour passed, and I suddenly heard Candy, my Sister-in-law, loudly cry out. She, along with other family members, were waiting in the hall next to my hospital room door. The second I heard Candy's cry, I knew my daughter had passed away. Although knowing in my heart and mind that my baby had died, I could not let myself except it. I was in denial and until I heard the words come from my Doctors mouth, in my mind she was still alive.

Then my worst fear happened. The door to my hospital room opened and my doctor came into my room. We all knew by the look on his face what had happened but I refused to hear him say the words. Before he could even open his mouth, I put my hand up in the air, and while crying I said, *"Please don't say it, I don't want to hear it."* Knowing what the doctor was about to say, my husband sat down on my bed. He held me in his arms, and we both cried as the doctor said, *"I'm so sorry to have to tell you this, but your daughter has just passed away."* He then went on to tell us that the ambulance from the University Hospital in Mississippi, was half way there when she died.

The doctor could have hit me in the head with a sledge hammer and it wouldn't have affected me any worse than the words that had just come out of his mouth! At that very moment, it felt like someone had reached inside my chest, jerked my heart out, threw it on the floor, and then jumped up and down on it. In the fifteen years I had been living on this earth, I had never experienced such heart ache and grief. To me, the weight of the whole world had just landed on my shoulders. I was completely and totally devastated! At that moment, my burden was too heavy to carry and I wanted my life over. I felt dying would be easier than having to go on living without her!

For the next few hours, after I had been told about her passing away, I buried my head in my pillow, and sobbed uncontrollably. My husband, mom, and family members tried to comfort me, but I was inconsolable. Nothing in this world was going to help the unbearable pain deep inside my heart and soul. My daughter was gone and nothing was going to bring her back! Through all the years of childhood abuse, none of it had ever hurt me as severely as losing her did. I have heard many times through the years that there's no greater heartache than the loss of your own child. Sad to say, I know how very true those words are.

After our daughter's funeral, and some time had passed by, Gary and I tried to pick up the pieces that were left of our lives and move on. Although Gary nor I ever fully recovered from her death, we did learn to live with it. Throughout our marriage God blessed Gary and me with three more beautiful children. He and I were married for seven years and have remained friends up to this day.

I would also like to mention that some years later, before my dad passed away, he humbled himself before God, and asked for my forgiveness many times. In the last ten years of his life, he and I were able to put the past behind us, and we had a good relationship at the time of his passing away.

CHAPTER TEN

MY LIFE TODAY

Even though I have lived through abuse in every aspect of the word, have been homeless, penniless, severely ill to the point of near death, and have suffered the greatest heart ache of all, the loss of a child, today my life is filled with much happiness and gratitude. I can honestly say that God has truly blessed my life. I have a wonderful husband, three loving children of my own, two step children, and a slew of grandkids. Although I am deeply enriched with all these blessings, I must confess, the road I have traveled throughout my life, by far has not been an easy one.

The severe abuse I was forced to live in throughout my childhood and teenage years seriously took its toll on me. Mentally and emotionally, the abuse had affected my judgment, or should I say lack of it, in men. By the time I met my husband Mark, I had already lived through four marriages gone bad. Mark and I were introduced on a blind date which had been arranged through a mutual friend of ours. For me, it was love at first sight! After years of abusive relationships and disastrous marriages I had finally met the man of my dreams. Mark's background was completely opposite of mine. He was raised by two loving parents and was well educated. Although we came from two very different walks of life, we have been inseparable since the day we met. With that said though, I can't say our life together has been smooth sailing, because I would be lying if I did. Like everyone else's life, our marriage too, has had its ups and downs. I can say though, with God's help, our marriage has only grown stronger, and our love deeper, with every challenge and obstacle we have had to resolve and overcome.

When I met Mark, I was working in a hospital as an insurance biller. I had been employed there for five years and really enjoyed my job. I had every intention of working there until I reached retirement age. About a year later, I began to notice I was having difficulties remembering my job tasks at work. I had soon filled the cubical I worked in with sticky notes to help me remember my daily work. My fellow coworkers had jokingly nick named me, "the queen of sticky notes." We would all laugh, and make jokes about aging and memory loss, but deep down inside I was truly concerned. Unknowingly to me, my supervisor had also noticed my forgetfulness. When my yearly evaluation came around for that year, my supervisor had given me a less than desirable score for my work performance. Due to the poor evaluation, I was put on probation and told my job was in jeopardy.

Fearful of losing my job, I went to my family PR actioner for help. After a thorough examination and me telling him about my childhood abuse, the loss of my first child, and four previous marriages, he diagnosed me with Post Traumatic Stress Disorder. He then took me off work indefinitely and recommended that I be evaluated by a psychologist. Even though at the time I didn't understand how crippling Post Traumatic Stress could be in someone's life, I was willing to do whatever was necessary to save my job.

My doctor then referred me to a psychologist, but due to not accepting my insurance, she in turn referred me to another psychologist whose name was Jennifer Kelly. There is no doubt in my mind that the events that led up to me meeting Jennifer was all in God's plan for my future. God used this very special Christian woman, to literally save my life. I say this because in the several years of counseling that I had with Jennifer there were a couple of times I truly wanted to give up on living. But God had other plans for me and through Jennifer he healed the scars from my past and gave me a reason to get up every morning. Jennifer has not only been my counselor who has helped me to accept and live with the darkest secrets of my life, but she has also been a very loving and loyal true friend. I was truly blessed when God placed her in my life and I will always be grateful to her for going above and beyond the call of duty to help me.

Because of the symptoms I was having, caused by Post Traumatic Stress Disorder, my doctor and psychologist considered me disabled and I was not allowed to return back to work. I loved my job at the hospital and having to give it up was very hard for me to accept. I had worked with the public my whole adult life and always excelled at each job I held. Being forced to give up a job that I really liked doing, because of my work performance was embracing and depressing to say the least. Then not having a time clock to punch every day and having so much time on my hands was also hard to get used to. But as time went on, I would come to understand why my having a full time job was no longer in God's plan for me. Losing my job was just God's way of bringing me one step closer to his plans for my future.

Because I knew what it felt like to be a homeless foster child in state custody, one of my goals in life was to be a foster parent if I was ever given the opportunity. Well, losing my job did just that. I now had the time and opportunity to take foster parenting classes and foster children.

The first year that Mark and I fostered, we were considered a level one home. Meaning the children we fostered had minimal to no problems at all. Then in our second year of fostering, we decided to have more training and become a level two home. Children with behavioral issues, or physical and mental disabilities, were placed in a level two home. Depending on the severity of the child's condition they could also be placed in a level three home or an institution. During the time that we were a level two home, I admit some of the children that were placed in our care, without a doubt, tried our patience. But if I could go back in time, I know without hesitation, I would choose to be a foster parent again. Being able to give these children a loving, safe home to live in was one of the most rewarding experiences I have ever had. It was also very therapeutic for me as well, but heart breaking at the same time. As I watched these children suffer from not being with their families, it would break my heart.

I remember one time being awakened in the middle of the night by one of our foster children. He was standing outside our bed room door crying. He was only five years old and had been awakened from having a bad nightmare. I quickly jumped out of bed, took him by the hand, and walked him into the living room. I sat down in our rocking chair, and as I held him in my arms, I rocked and sang to him. The memory of my daddy, doing this same thing with me, many years before that night, came rushing back through my mind like a gush of wind. When I asked him why he was crying, he told me about his nightmare and how much he missed and wanted his mommy. My heart ached for this little boy's pain. I wanted desperately to take his heart ache away, but I knew the only thing that would ease his pain was to be back with his mother. While I held him, as he cried for his mommy to be there, my own demon's from the past came rushing back to haunt me. I began to think back in time to when I was five years old and how I, too, had cried for my mommy to come and save me. With every fiber of my body I could feel anger and frustration in not being able to mend this little boy's broken heart. Like a recording, thoughts of no child at any age should ever have to experience this severe grief and heart ache, kept playing over and over in my mind.

I then started to reflect on my relationship with my own mom. She was very domineering with me, and still to that day, blamed me for the past abuse by my dad. With sly remarks she would go out of her way to hurt my feelings or make me feel guilty over what had happen. My brother Roy was now her favorite and believe me, the difference she showed between the two of us was very obvious to everyone.

Roy by far was no angel. Not only had he abused me as a child, and also as a teenager, but later in life, he also had a problem with other family members. When my mom found this out she stated that it was their fault, if it even happened at all. It appeared that no matter what Roy did, in my mom eyes he, could do no wrong. As far as my mom was concerned, everyone was lying, or if Roy did anything wrong, it was the other person's fault. I have only mentioned this about Roy just to shed light on the partiality my mom showed between the two of us. It seemed the harder I tried to please her, the meaner she treated me. I was the one that had been abused, but yet I was the one she resented and blamed. Having these thoughts run through my mind, as I held this little boy in my arms, made me more determined than ever to help any abused child that I could.

During this same time that Mark and I were fostering children, my mom became very ill and was admitted into the hospital. Although my feelings were deeply hurt over the way she had treated me throughout the years, I still loved her very much. She was my mom, and I felt a sense of gratitude toward her, for giving me a home to live in when I was homeless. I also felt in my heart that she had raised me and was a good mom through my adolescent years. When I found out that she was in the hospital, without hesitation, I planned to stay with her until she was released. My dad had passed away several years before and Roy lived out of state so the only person left to be with her was me.

Mark, myself, and our foster child that we were caring for at the time went to the hospital to see my mom. While we were there my mom asked us if we would go to her house and pick up some personal belongings that she would need while in the hospital. We told her of course we would, and left our foster child behind to keep her company while we were gone.

While Mark and I were searching for what she had asked us to bring her, we stumbled on her will. I decided to read it but wished I hadn't by the time I was finished. I knew my mom had a lot of resentment and bitterness towards me, but I didn't realize just how much until then. She had taken me out of her will. I was stunned, my feelings hurt, and completely at a loss for words. I looked up at Mark, handed him my mom's will, and told him to read it. After he read the will he looked at me and said, "Well, now you know." To me it wasn't about her money. It was knowing how she really felt about me. All I had ever wanted from my mom was her love and approval. I was crushed. The woman who had raised me, that I truly loved and had called my mom, wanted me to have nothing of hers after she passed away. Because I was so shocked and hurt to know that she had taken me out of her will, I wasn't able to talk to her about it at that time.

My mom remained in the hospital for three weeks and during that time she was diagnosed with pancreatic cancer. Due to the severity of the disease, she would need constant care after being released to go home. Although knowing that I had been disinherited, I basically moved in with her anyway, and never left her side. Mark and I took care of my mom in shifts. I had the day shift, and because Mark was used to working nights with his jobs, he took the night shift.

During this time, my mom and I did eventually talk about her will. She told me that she didn't realize how much I loved her and she wanted to change what she had written in her will. It's truly amazing how with some people, it takes facing death before they can really appreciate the blessings God gave them.

Roy was also traveling back and forth during this time to help with my mom. On one of his trips to Tennessee, while Roy and I were both in the room, my mom told each one of us what she wanted us to have after she was gone. I was more than grateful to receive anything that my mom wanted me to have. But what meant the most to me was to know that she had a change of heart before she passed away.

Even though I was sad about my mom's passing away, I was also relieved. The turmoil that had been between us for so many years had been a heavy burden to carry. The strained relationship we had not only affected my life, but also my husband and childrens' lives. There were many times my mom would go through my children, and even Mark, just to get at me. For the first time in my whole entire life, I truly felt a sense of freedom from abuse. I would no longer have to force myself to be around Roy just to please my mom. Also, my days of being verbally, mentally, and emotionally mistreated by my mom were finally over. I knew from this point forward my life would change and I would be a much happier person.

About a year after my mom passed away, our foster children went back to live with their parents. During this same time, the economy was starting to get bad and Mark was laid off from his job. We neither one wanted to move away from our children and grandchildren, but due to the lack of jobs where we lived, we decided to relocate. Mark's brother lived in Kentucky, so we decided to move there in hopes of finding work. After about six months of continuous job searching, Mark was finally hired as a supervisor at a manufacturing company. Just when we thought our lives were back on track again and we would survive the economy melt down, I became very ill.

For four straight months I went from one doctor to another hoping to get answers as to what was wrong with me. Each doctor would perform a series of tests in which the results would always come back normal. When the doctors couldn't find a medical reason as to why I was so sick, they determined my diagnosis of post-traumatic stress disorder was the culprit and the cause of all my health problems. I was then referred to another psychiatrist to be treated for the physical health problems I was having. In my mind I knew my health issues had nothing to do with PTSD and being referred to a psychiatrist for physical sickness made no since to me at all. But I was desperate for help, and by that point, I was willing to do whatever I had to in order to get better.

Naturally, because my test had come back normal, and my doctor had referred me to this psychiatrist, she too agreed that my health issues all stemmed from my PTSD. Before I knew it, I was on so much psychiatric medication that it was making me emotionally and mentally unstable. After a couple of times contemplating suicide and a few trips to the mental ward in the hospital, I knew the medication was driving me crazy. I then decided I would stop taking all the medication that had been prescribed to me, and if nothing else, hope that I would at least get my brain back.

Stopping that medication was one of the best things I had ever done for myself. After a couple of weeks of being off the medicine, I could tell that mentally I was starting to feel much better. About this same time, the physical health issues that I had been having also started to fade away. I never did find out what caused me to be so physically ill, but I was sure grateful to God that I was on the road to recovery.

After a year and a half of living in Kentucky, Mark once again was laid off from his job. Again, we were stuck with the same dilemma of whether to relocate or continue to live in Kentucky and search for another job there. After putting our heads together and discussing our situation Mark and I decided we would move back to Tennessee, to be near our children and grandchildren. It worked out really well for us because at the time my daughter was working for a temporary agency and was able to put Mark to work our first day back in Tennessee. Of course, this left most of the unpacking for me to do, but I was just so happy to be near my children again that I didn't mind a bit.

About six months after moving back to Tennessee I heard about a child advocacy program called CASA (Court Appointed Special Advocate). After learning more about this program, I knew this was something I very much wanted to be a part of. Even though I loved being a foster parent, I felt becoming a CASA was my real calling. After talking it over with Mark, he too decided to be a CASA, and we both took the training classes together. After we completed our training, we were then sworn in as Volunteer Court Appointed Special Advocates by Judge Hudson. After being sworn in, I was ready to go to work and anxiously waited to be assigned my first case.

One day during this same time period, while out shopping in town, I ran into a social worker whose name is Reba. Mark and I met Reba and had worked with her when we were foster parents. While we were talking, Reba mentioned that she had been trying to locate Mark and me, but didn't know where we were living. She then went on to say that she wanted to talk to us about taking in a young girl whose name was Randi. Reba explained that Randi had recently turned nineteen, and as long as she remained in college, she was considered post custody by the state. Because of my passion to help children, I eagerly told her I would be interested in hearing more about her. I then gave Reba my new address and phone number and told her to call me so we could schedule a time to get together.

After our meeting with Reba, and getting more information about Randi, Mark and I asked her to bring Randi to our house so we could all meet. After meeting Randi, I could tell right away that she was a very pleasant person and well mannered. Mark and I both agreed that we would let Randi move in and do whatever we could to help her. Randi ended up living with us for about nine months. In those nine months, Mark and I both grew to love Randi and became very attached to her. I remember crying on the day she moved out from our home and making her promise to stop by often to visit. To this day Mark and I consider Randi our daughter and love her dearly.

A few months after Randi had moved out, I once again became extremely ill. This time though, it would nearly take my life. I had come down with a really bad cold and had been placed on antibiotics that my doctor had prescribed for me. Although I was taking medication, I continued to get worse and on April 13, 2010, I was admitted in the hospital with a diagnosis of double pneumonia. I was placed on steroids, stronger antibiotics, and a high intake level of oxygen. With each day that passed, it appeared that I was just getting worse instead of better. My doctor then consulted with a lung specialist, and together, they soon realized that what they thought was typical pneumonia might very well be some other type of lung disease. They had based this decision on the fact that I been diagnosed with having Lupus a few months before being admitted in the hospital.

An MRI and CAT scan of my lungs was ordered, and the results showed that the disease that had first appeared in the bottom of my lungs had now spread throughout both my lungs. After seeing the results of these test, my doctor asked for my permission to do a lung biopsy. He explained that if they could find out the type of disease which had taken over my lungs they would be able to treat it better. He also explained that because I was on such a high intake level of oxygen, they would have to wait until they could get the oxygen level lower. He stated that my lungs were too weak to hold up through the surgery, but as soon as they had a window of opportunity they would to the biopsy.

I had been in the hospital about ten days when my oxygen intake level was finally low enough to have the lung biopsy procedure performed. In order to get to this point though, I was not permitted to get out of my hospital bed for anything. Even sitting up in my bed to eat would cause me to need more oxygen. Also by this point I was starting to get delirious due to being on pain medication and the lack of oxygen to my brain. I was so out of touch with what was going on around me that to this day I still have no memory of the surgeries.

When I woke up from having the lung biopsy I was in severe pain. I didn't realize that a chest tube had been inserted in my right lung during surgery. Immediately my nurse told me about the chest tube, and my need to lie still. Shortly after I had awakened, my doctor came in my room to check on me. He told me that during surgery, my right lung collapsed and this was the reason for the chest tube. Two days later, I was taken back to surgery to have the chest tube removed only to have it put back in the very next day. I was told that the biopsy procedure had caused my lungs to start bleeding and this was the reason for the second surgery. At this point, not only were my lungs bleeding, but also my bowels and kidneys were bleeding as well. Simply put, I was bleeding to death.

When I was admitted in the hospital, I signed a paper stating that I would not accept a blood transfusion should I need one. My reasons for this was because of my religious belief at the time, and I was also fearful of contracting Aids. I also felt that having a blood transfusion was something that I wouldn't need to be concerned about anyway. Little did I know that having a blood transfusion would be the very thing I would be faced with in order to save my life.

I had been in the hospital by this time about two weeks. One night my doctor came in my room to inform me that my blood count was extremely low. He stated that it was so dangerously low that without a blood transfusion I would not live through the night. He also said that he was very aware of my refusal to accept blood, and respected my religious beliefs. But he then went further and said in order to live I had no choice but to accept the blood.

I can't even express in words my feelings at that moment, other than to say I was totally shocked! Like so many other people in this world, it was now my turn to stare death in the face. I was only forty nine years old at the time, and all I could think about was that I was entirely too young to die. I also thought about how it wouldn't be fair to my husband or children to let myself die, due to my own religious beliefs. But then on the other hand, even though I had no desire to die, my religious convictions were just as strong as my will to live.

Then there was my husband and doctor by my side, both encouraging me to accept the blood transfusion. I was totally confused at this point and unsure of my own feelings. So I did the only thing I knew to do, and that was to close my eyes and pray to my Heavenly Father. As I prayed, asking God to help me make the right decision, I also prayed for His will to be done, and not mine. Then instantly I felt a sense of calmness come over me and I was no longer afraid. When I opened my eyes, I suddenly found myself alone in my hospital room, with Jesus. I knew without a doubt that I was with Jesus because this was not my first time to have a spiritual encounter with Him. Then by using telepathy, He began talking to me and said, "It's not about religion, it's about your relationship with God." Also at that same time, Jesus showed me visions of different things which made me appreciate more than ever the gift of life. Then what seemed to me, in a blink of an eye, Jesus was out of my sight, and my husband and doctor were back in the room with me. Instantly I felt the gift of God's Holy Spirit totally consume my entire body. The feeling I had was like being reborn again, and God had just given me a new lease on life. I was completely overwhelmed with feelings of peacefulness, and gratitude. Without any further hesitation I was compelled to tell the doctor that I would accept the blood transfusion. After being given five liters of blood, my blood count went back to normal.

By this time though, I had been in the hospital, confined to a bed, for nearly a month. Lying in bed for this length of time, without getting any exercise, played havoc with my digestive system. The next evening after my blood transfusions, I was awakened with severe stomach pain. The pain was so severe that I remember crying and telling my nurse that my stomach was going to burst wide open at any second. She called for the doctor, and the next thing I knew, I was getting my stomach pumped out. For any of you readers that have never had your stomach pumped, believe me, *it's definitely something you never want to have done!* Once my stomach issues were treated, I slowly started to recover and was sent home a few days later.

I know there are people in this world who don't believe in extraordinary near death experiences, and that's okay too. But as for me, I have no doubts at all that for some of us, this miracle really does happen. *While I laid in my hospital bed near death, I was blessed by God to be spiritually reborn and was fully emerged with His Holy Spirit.* I don't know why God chose to intervene in my life, but I do know there are millions of people just like me in dire need of experiencing His presence, love and grace. This amazing and privileged experience has changed my life forever. I no longer take life for granted. *Instead, with each passing day, I cherish every breath that God allows me to take. I truly appreciate, the miracle of life, and thank God each morning that I wake up for this precious gift.*

I know wholeheartedly, that God has a plan for my life. I say this because I have also survived two strokes that I had in May of 2011. I am alive and living with only minor side effects from the strokes. Even I'm not sure that I would believe all the events of my life's story to be true had I not personally lived through each and every day of them. I can honestly say though, I now understand why I suffered the childhood abuse as well as other trials and tribulations throughout my life. It was all included in God's plan, to mold me into the person that I am today. My life experiences, although some at times have seemed unbearable, have made me a better person. God has truly blessed me and I want nothing more out of life than to serve Him, as well as others. I pray God will allow me to continue as a voice for all abused and neglected children worldwide. Also, until my dying breath, I will always be a witness to His unconditional love and mercy due to the Grace that He has bestowed on my life.

With that said, I can now say after several months in the making, reliving emotional turmoil with many tears shed, sleepless nights with haunting nightmares returning, and many said prayers, my life's story is finally finished. Thank you, God, for the lessons learned and the spiritual wisdom and insight I have gained as I traveled the road of life you planned for me from the beginning.

ABOUT THE AUTHOR

Patsy married Mark Giddings on May 28, 2005. They have five children and fifteen grandchildren, and now reside in Cookeville, TN. Because of Patsy and Mark's love for children and due to the severe child abuse Patsy suffered as a child, they soon became foster parents, doing this for two years, before becoming volunteer court appointed special advocates (CASA). Their passion runs deep and personal in a determination to help abused children. It is the reason that she and Mark became CASA Volunteers. It is also the reason she went on to become a voice of advocacy, giving public lectures to bring awareness of the desperate need existing in modern day America, to protect our children.

But in her lectures, Patsy explains how her dependence on God was lifesaving, as she struggled to live through one nightmare after another and the important lessons it holds about the meaning and purpose of our lives. She is committed to increasing awareness of God's presence, love and grace and tells how God brought her to where she is today—saved, rescued, and at peace.

These are some of the places that she has attended as a CASA spokesperson:

- Child Advocacy Days in Nashville, Tennessee. (Spoke with Senator Charlotte Burks pertaining to the CASA Program)

- Cookeville Free Will Baptist Church, Ladies Group, in Cookeville, Tennessee.

- Yankee Town Free Will Baptist Church, Sparta, Tennessee.

- First Baptist Church, Livingston, Tennessee.

- Interviewed twice for CASA Program, by WHUB Radio Show, in Cookeville, Tennessee.

- Overton County, Child Abuse Blue Ribbon Memorial Ceremony, in Livingston, Tennessee.

- Tennessee CASA Network Training/Director's Meeting, in Murfreesboro, Tennessee.

- August 03, 2012 Became a Member of the Upper Cumberland Council on Children and Youth (UCCCY). A Regional Program of the Tennessee Commission on Children and Youth (TCCY).

I have written my life's story in this book, not for pity, or vengefulness in any kind of way. My hope is that this book will be used and placed in the libraries of all child advocacy programs, especially CASA, as a tool in helping abused and neglected children worldwide. I also hope it will bring awareness that adoption doesn't necessarily mean a child is safe!

Fan Mail Address:

Patsy Giddings
P.O. Box 2004
Cookeville, TN 38501

Phone: (931) 881-8305
E-Mail: pattigiddings@gmail.com

To request Patsy for speaking engagements, interviews, or book signings, please contact,

Chris Mullens, Public Relations Manager at:

Office Phone: (903) 833-5185
E-Mail: pattigiddings@gmail.com
Address: P.O. Box 1201 Canton, TX 75103

BOOK REVIEWS

"A compelling story of abuse and neglect that I could not put down . . . From Sandy's parent's abuse and neglect, to multiple foster home abuses, Sandy was moved from foster home to foster home always hoping and waiting for that perfect home. Even when she thought she had found the perfect home, the perfect mom that became a nightmare too. Sandy through her anger, fears and tears, managed to find her strength through God, making her the strong, passionate, loving person she is today. This strength has given her the resolve to be a loving wife, mother, foster parent and a strong Advocate for abused and neglected children that she serves. I am proud to work with Patsy (Sandy) and know that she has the best interest at heart for each and every child she serves. Sandy's story is a story that no child should ever have to live or tell, but sadly hundreds of thousands of children do. A must read for hope and inspiration for all . . . Rita Turnipseed, Volunteer Coordinator UCHRA, Putnam, County CASA

*****

"I came to know Patsy through the . . . Court Appointed Special Advocates program. We had met in various meetings and I was drawn to her as a person of Godly character. We attended a speaker training meeting and that is when I heard a story about a child named Sandy. Patsy spoke of horrific abuse that Sandy had lived through and this was the reason that she became an advocate for CASA. At the end of her story she stated that Sandy was her . . .

WOW! TEARS and compassion came flooding forth. In April 2012, during . . . Child Abuse Awareness Month, Overton, County, didn't have a spokesperson. I asked our team if I could have Patsy speak at the . . . Blue Ribbon Ceremony. This took place April 26, 2012. At that time only CASA personnel had heard her story. I was apprehensive about the community's reaction to her story. But Patsy approached the podium with confidence and assurance. Her mission was to tell her story and the reason why she volunteers as an advocate for abused and neglected children . . . Her story inspired many people and even brought grown men to tears. This changed the course of the program. Mayor Curtis Hayes, asked Pastor Don Cobb, to pray for the abused and neglected children. Because Patsy was willing to come forward and tell her story, she was approached to write her story in a book. As you read about Sandy, and the life that God protected, you will see a wonderful woman named Patsy emerge. Mark Giddings, her husband, supports and cherishes his wife. I love these two people and wish them the best as this book goes out to touch many lives . . . Rondi R. Van Vorce, CASA Volunteer Coordinator, Overton, County, TN

*****

"It doesn't take long for anyone who reads her book or listens to her speak to realize that author Patsy Giddings, is not only a survior but a humble and compassionate person. She lives her life to educate individuals and groups regarding the realities of child abuse. I first met Ms. Giddings when she came to me for counseling. As a Licensed Clinical Social Worker, I knew if she would get relief from her nightmares, daily, torturous, flashbacks and failed relationships, she was facing long and painful therapy sessions. Ms. Giddings began an extremely angry person but soon transferred that anger to an engry that would bring determination to heal. She accepted Christ as her Lord and Savior which further increased her healing. As she experienced her own healing, her compassion for children experiencing abuse began to grow. She sought opportunities in her community to help these children . . . My life has been changed for knowing her. I admire and respect

the courage she has demonstrated and turned a hopeless life into hope . . . Jennifer Kelly, L.C.S.W.

*****

"We live in a world of hurting people and I am very thankful to Patsy that she had the courage and caring to share her story of a childhood that only a severely, neglected and abused child could experience. Not only a must read for those who work with abused children, but also a great training tool for volunteers who work with these same children. Also contains great spiritual insight! . . . David R. Ayers, Executive Director, CASA of Campbell County, TN

*****

"It is hard to understand how anyone could survive the ordeal that Sandy endured. No human should have to be as brutally abused as Sandy was. She was abused by her own family and then, by the foster home's that she was sent to. After reading this book, it makes me more aware of why Patsy is so passionate to help the abused and neglected children—first as a foster parent (a good one I may add), and then as a CASA Advocate . . . This book will keep you involved from beginning to end—first with tears of sadness and then tears of happiness, when you see how she has not only survived, but has become a wonderful woman. I am blessed to have worked with Patsy through the CASA program . . . Judy Greenwood, UCHRA CASA Program Director, Putnam, Cumberland, Overton and Smith Counties/TN

❧ JOHN BORGSTEDT ❧

John Borgstedt is a native Texan with a special love for nature, blue skies overhead, and a unique brand of protective maturity for the young and innocent. His flight and fight for survival throughout his earlier years instilled a heartfelt desire to help others. After much contemplation on how to accomplish this goal, John felt he must share the unspeakable horrors that he had survived throughout his childhood. Perhaps the exposure of truth would heal and mend the society that had failed him.

With ferocious tenacity, John faces and conquers the challenges of flashbacks of long-buried memories, exposing deep, dark wounds of physical and emotional atrocities every time he shares his remarkable story of overcoming insurmountable odds in life as a child. Amid the love and support of his devoted wife, Virginia, the two never waver from the mission to improve the life of child victims of abuse.

Mr. Borgstedt is a noted motivational speaker for young and old alike. From school children and faculty to correctional institutions with hardened criminals to devout Christian church groups, John's message of hope, love, and determination touches the hearts and minds of his audience. Indeed, fans and followers of John Borgstedt patiently await the day that his ultimate dream and goal of establishing a boys ranch becomes a reality.

This warrior for 'right' is not a quitter!

* * * * *

To request John for speaking engagements, interviews, or book signings OR to order books or DVDs, please contact John at:
Phone: 903-833-5185
E-Mail: johnborgstedt@aol.com
For books: Visit the website at www.iloveyoumom.net
For DVDs: Visit the website at www.iloveyoumommovie.com
Fan Mail Address: John Borgstedt, P.O. Box 1201, Canton, Texas 75103

"I Love You, Mom keeps readers riveted, as John Borgstedt describes his childhood journey through the mine fields of horrible beatings by his own parents who kept him overdosed on behavior altering drugs, as well as abuse and molestation in numerous state homes in which he was placed from a very early age. After escaping a murder attempt by his own mother, it's truly miraculous that John has obtained victory over his past and now uses his own story to reach others who are hurting with a message of hope." – Timna Rutledge, Editor, The Northeast Texan

"John Borgstedt holds nothing back in this true story of faith and change. It's one of the most powerful stories of survival ever told." Cindy Aguirre-Herrera – Seguin Daily News.

* * * * *

"As a work of fiction, "I love you Mom, please don't break my heart" would be the kind of novel that leaves you up a little longer at night wondering what would happen if the story were true. Knowing that John Borgstedt's story isn't fiction, however, breaks your heart for John and all those who suffer through such circumstances. Thank God, literally, for John's ability to tell this story with such honesty and poignancy so that others may not turn a blind eye to such horrors. But this isn't a story of horror; it's one of hope!" Jayson Larson – Athens Daily Review

* * * * *

"In I love you mom: Please don't break my heart, John Borgstedt tells of his young life and the abuse he suffered at the hand of his mother. It is a difficult to read tale, but the story does not end there. He is a survivor who visualized a better future for himself in public speaking forums at prisons, boy's camps, and even in the courtroom as an advocate for child safety." Janice Ernest, Editor – "WhileUWait" magazine

* * * * *

Order ***John's*** *new movie at*

johnborgstedt@aol.com

God Bless You Little Ones
by... John Borgstedt

God bless you little ones, everywhere
All alone in a world,
Of so much to spare
Still there is no shelter
No one to care...

God bless you little ones, everywhere
So alone, so forgotten,
It is indeed unfair
Longing for love
Someone to care...

Crying tears not of your doing
Amid life's disarray
Committing no crime
Yet punished this way
Fighting for survival
In endless days...

What happened to our human race?
Has not empathy earned a place?

We don't see your face
We don't hear your cries
Your fear, heartache, pains
Little ones whispering 'Why'...
Turning our heads
Time swiftly moves by
Too many little ones across this land
Bearing burdens too great to withstand

I hear now your cry,
Your pain I feel
My love pours forth
No longer concealed
And I pray
God bless you little ones...

* * * * *

To read more of John's inspirational story as a victim of child abuse and his days of incarceration, read his book, _I LOVE YOU, MOM – Please Don't Break My Heart._